W9-DFT-070

WITHDRAWN

89-1837

PR
3316
.A4
Z78
1987

Women Writers

Fanny Burney

Judy Simons

Gramley Library
Salem College
Winston-Salem, NC 27108

BARNES & NOBLE BOOKS
TOTOWA, NEW JERSEY

© Judy Simons 1987

First published in the USA 1987 by
BARNES & NOBLE BOOKS
81 ADAMS DRIVE
TOTOWA, NEW JERSEY 07512

ISBN 0–389–20693–8
ISBN 0–389–20694–6 (Pbk)

Printed in Hong Kong

Library of Congress Cataloging-in-Publication Data
Simons, Judy.
Fanny Burney.
Bibliography: p.
Includes index.
1. Burney, Fanny, 1752–1840—Criticism and interpretation.
I. Title.
PR3316.A4Z78   1987   823'.6   86–22291
ISBN 0–389–20693–8
ISBN 0–389–20694–6 (pbk.)

Contents

Editors' Preface

The study of women's writing has been long neglected by a male critical establishment both in academic circles and beyond. As a result, many women writers have either been unfairly neglected, or have been marginalised in some way, so that their true influence and importance has been ignored. Other women writers have been accepted by male critics and academics, but on terms which seem, to many women readers of this generation, to be false or simplistic. In the past the internal conflicts involved in being a woman in a male-dominated society have been largely ignored by readers of both sexes, and this has affected our reading of women's work. The time has come for a serious re-assessment of women's writing in the light of what we understand today.

This series is designed to help in that re-assessment. All the books are written by women, because we believe that men's understanding of feminist critique is only, at best, partial. And besides, men have held the floor quite long enough.

Eva Figes
Adele King

Editors' Preface

EVA FIGES
Adele King

1 Fanny Burney's Life

Shortly after the publication of *Evelina*, Fanny Burney was sitting alone in the library of Mrs Thrale's house at Streatham, when suddenly the door opened and a gentleman walked in. Flustered, Burney hurriedly tried to hide the book she had been browsing through, because, as she later commented, 'I dreaded being thought studious and affected'. The book she had chosen as diversion for those idle moments was the latest translation of Cicero's *Laelius*. Perhaps no incident better illustrates the tensions that existed between Burney's private inclinations and her public face. Deeply reflective, sharply observant and a natural highbrow, she was nonetheless constantly terrified of being noticed as 'different'. The opinion of others was always the most powerful influence on her as, torn between a critical attitude towards her society and her need to be accepted by it, she struggled to suppress her own originality and to conform to the approved mould of womanly diffidence. In this, she exemplifies the paradoxical situation of women of her time.

Throughout the eighteenth century, educational opportunities for girls had been expanding. Fanny Burney was born in 1752 and by the time she was growing up there were girls' schools which offered academic subjects as part of the syllabus – arithmetic, grammar, history, geography and French (although it was rare to find all these in the same establishment). Yet still Lady Mary Wortley Montagu was forced to admit to her daughter that 'the ultimate end of your

education was to make you a good wife'.[1] Here in a nutshell is
one of the central anomalies of the situation. For despite
widening horizons, young women found that their social
leverage was more limited than ever before. The newly
prosperous middle classes wanted their women to appear
leisured and delicate. Domestic tasks were carried out by
servants and many women had little to do except be
ornamental. In the heavily male oriented society, marriage
was the only respectable occupation open to them and, if they
wished to guarantee their future security, they had to
conform to the compliant stereotype that men had created for
them. Instead of being able to exercise their newly awakened
intellects, girls were warned to hide any evidence of their
having minds at all, in case a display of mental power should
frighten off a prospective husband. Dr John Gregory's
famous advice to women, 'If you happen to have any
learning, keep it a profound secret, especially from the men',[2]
was echoed and re-echoed by parents who recognised that, as
Jane Austen so acidly noted, 'imbecility in females' was a
great advantage. A girl had to realise that 'what is most
absolutely necessary, is to conceal whatever learning she
attains with as much solicitude as she would hide
crookedness or lameness',[3] and although occasional clever
women were admired, it was only on the clear understanding
that they were exceptions rather than the rule. As Lord
Lyttleton wrote of the scholar, Catherine Macaulay, 'Once in
every age I would like such a woman to appear as proof that
genius is not confined to sex . . . but . . . at the same time
. . . you'll pardon me, we want no more than *one* Mrs.
Macaulay'.[4]

But women's learning and articulacy was inevitably
becoming more widespread and by the 1770s the topic of
women's nature and capacities had become the subject of
vigorous debate in intellectual circles. The sentimentalist
school of thought, with its emphasis on the value of private
feeling, suggested that women were particularly well

equipped to shine as emotional luminaries. Their natural qualities were considered to be those which were the products of a feeling heart; tenderness, compassion, intuitive sympathy, qualities which bypassed the need for judgement or rational thought. These characteristics, which operated primarily on the level of personal rather than public relationships, endorsed the conservative view of woman's true role as supportive and domestic. 'Woman's sphere is the house', insisted Samuel Richardson's Sir Charles Grandison, and 'Subordination is the natural sphere in which we were intended to move'[5] agreed Charlotte Palmer, unable to conceive any alternative to the contemporary creed of male dominance.

Early feminist writers, however, were forcefully proposing a different view. As early as 1694, Mary Astell's *A Serious Proposal to the Ladies* had argued that women were rational beings, capable of independent thought and action, and these ideas were now extended into what many saw as much more politically subversive directions. Lady Mary Wortley Montagu's attitude of resigned acceptance, ' 'tis always the fate of women to obey', was being challenged by both men and women committed to the idea that such a condition was no longer inevitable. Most expressions of feminist sympathy were at this stage confined to fiction, and emerged through the portrayal of active and dynamic female characters in novels aimed at a largely female readership, but towards the end of the century a series of explicit feminist polemics appeared, which broadcast the scepticism about male supremacy and about previously unquestioned views of relations between the sexes. That women were increasingly educated, literate and thoughtful was undeniable, a fact that many traditionalists found deeply disturbing. Wistfully, Dr Johnson 'well remembered when a woman who could spell a common letter was regarded as all accomplished, but now they vie with the men in everything.'[6] Such progressiveness clearly made him most uncomfortable and it was in such an atmosphere of uncertainty about women's status that Frances Burney grew up.

Born in 1752, Burney's very life as well as her writing expressed the confusions of the contemporary scene and the difficulties of being a woman at a time when the problems of forming an identity were so unclear. She was the fourth child in what was to become a large and boisterous family. Her mother, Esther, died when Fanny was ten – significantly Burney's heroines are all without a mother's guidance – leaving six surviving children and five years later her father remarried a Mrs Allen, a wealthy, attractive widow with three children of her own. In 1760 the Burneys had moved from the quiet country life of King's Lynn, Norfolk, to London and it was in the ferment of England's social and intellectual capital that Fanny Burney was to spend her formative years. Her father, Charles Burney, on his way to becoming an eminent, respected musician, had an energetic, untiring mind, coupled with enormous personal charm. He attracted fashionable pupils, quickly gained entrance to the most cultured society London had to offer and soon became something of a celebrity among the influential intelligentsia. The Burney household was often filled with laughter and activity, with witty conversation and lively, stimulating personalities. The celebrated actor, David Garrick, was a close family friend who spent hours entertaining the Burney children, encouraging them to develop their talents for observation and mimicry. They saw him at the theatre in tragic and comic roles and then watched him re-enact the parts for them at home, parts which Fanny in particular could imitate with outstanding accuracy. It was perhaps from Garrick that she first derived the idea of performance, an idea which was to penetrate her whole concept of living. Life for Burney was to become a series of roles, public performances which concealed the true self beneath, allowing only aspects of her real personality to emerge unchecked.

Collectively, the Burneys were an extraordinarily talented

family. The eldest son, James, made his career in the navy, where he reached the rank of Rear Admiral, having experienced among other adventures the dangers and excitements of Captain Cook's expeditions. Fanny's second brother, Charles, a brilliant theological student, rose to eminence in his profession, became chaplain to George III and was awarded the degree of Doctor of Divinity. Both Susan and Esther Burney, Fanny's sisters, were remarkably accomplished women, excelling in music, art and literature. Susan especially, always Fanny's closest confidante, wrote fine journals and letters, while their half-sister, Sarah, became a successful novelist, with four published novels to her credit.

Yet, during her early adolescence, Fanny, who was to become the most acclaimed of them all, was the odd one out. Painfully shy, she hid her gifts beneath a cloak of modesty whenever she was in unfamiliar company. Her childhood alternated between times of intense noise and activity in an animated household crowded with young people, family, friends and miscellaneous visitors of varying social ranks and long periods of solitude left to her own devices, when her father was travelling or working in his study and her brothers and sisters were away at school. Fanny Burney herself never had any sustained formal education. 'She was wholly unnoticed in the nursery for any talents or quickness of study',[7] complained her father, who consequently took little notice of his daughter's early progress. At eight she did not even know her alphabet but by the age of twelve, self-taught, she was roaming her father's impressive library, devouring books of history, essays, sermons and moral tracts, works which were to provide her with a clear ethical framework for her own conduct and her writing.

From this exceptional upbringing emerged an exceptional woman, although those who met her in company would hardly have thought so. Publicly, she always maintained the demeanour appropriate to eighteenth-century expectations

of women's behaviour, and she spoke out strongly against
any deviation from those standards. When her close friend,
the widowed Mrs Thrale, decided to marry Gabriel Piozzi,
her Italian music master, Burney was amongst those most
shocked by the open acknowledgement of passion. She
argued keenly against the marriage. 'All is at stake', she
wrote urgently to Mrs Thrale, attempting to dissuade her
from what she saw as a disastrous step. '– & for what? – a
gratification that no man can *esteem*, not even he for whom
you feel it.' Male approbation was as always the criterion
which guided her views and Mrs Thrale never forgave her for
what she interpreted as callousness and disloyalty. Despite
such a stance, however, Fanny Burney was conscious of a
tension between the pressures of the conventional world and
her own impulses to independence and she refused to accept,
even when young, many of the social attitudes that were
assumed to be automatic for a woman of her class. In her
early diary, she vowed repeatedly that she would never
marry. 'Singleness therefore be mine, with peace of mind and
liberty', she declared vehemently. When other girls of her
age saw marriage as their irrevocable duty, or even as their
means of escape from the tyranny of their parents, Burney
saw it only as an obstruction. Yet the marriage market was
the goal of most young women's training and all their
education was designed to increase their desirability as
ornament and childbearer. Marriage brought financial
security to women but equally it brought a degree of social
freedom. A young woman who failed to catch a husband was
likely to be patronised or ignored but, worse, was
condemned to spending the rest of her life dependent on her
parents' income and limited by their chaperonage. The
stereotype old maid was caricatured mercilessly – 'tall,
raw-boned, aukward, flat-chested and stooping'[8] one writer
described her – a natural butt for ridicule. Yet celibacy held
no fears for Burney. Even as a young girl, with what one
might imagine to be the romantic aspirations of adolescence,

she was unimpressed by the attractions of husband hunting. She valued her liberty of mind, a quality she felt could be seriously compromised by that inhibiting institution, marriage. Although she was modest, there is no evidence to suggest that she was cold towards men or nervous of competing with her more vivacious sisters. Neither was she neglected by masculine attention, despite her reticence and quiet manner. When she was twenty-two she rejected a pressing offer of marriage from a Mr Barlow, a most eligible suitor, and persisted in her refusal, in the face of warnings from her friends of the dreadful dangers of spinsterhood. 'Consider', pleaded her mentor, the adored 'Daddy' Crisp, 'the situation of an unprotected, unprovided woman', but she remained resolute. Her dictum was maintained that 'the most dignified thing for an exalted female must be to die an old maid'. Unworried by the associations of neglect and aridity, she saw the single state as the only certain means of keeping her integrity.

Constantly aware of her position in a world where male approval was the seal of success, Burney was reliant on two central sources of praise, her father and his good friend, Samuel Crisp, dubbed by the Burney children 'Daddy' Crisp. These two men became for her the ultimate in male perfection, her personal symbols of authority. Together, they watched, encouraged and scolded her and created for her a framework which was both to release and to limit her creative energies. It was Samuel Crisp who first recognised her spontaneous talent and literary potential and who accordingly helped her form her writing style. 'There is no fault in an epistolary correspondence like stiffness and study', he shrewdly advised her. 'Dash away whatever comes uppermost; the sudden sallies of the imagination clap'd down on paper, just as they arise.' He was however also responsible for impressing on her the fear of criticism which was never to leave her and which inhibited her later working methods. For Fanny Burney the act of writing clearly fulfilled the task

of reconciling her reticence with her imaginative energy. In
March 1768 she began writing a lengthy diary. She had
previously written most of a novel, *The History of Caroline
Evelyn*, which she had dutifully burnt with other scribblings,
an action which she later explained.

> So early was I impressed myself with ideas that fastened
> degradation to this class of composition, that at the age of
> adolescence, I struggled against the propensity, which
> even in childhood, even from the moment I could hold a
> pen, had impelled me with its toils; and on my fifteenth
> birthday, I made so resolute a conquest over an inclination
> at which I blushed, that I had always kept secret, that I
> committed to flames whatever up to that moment I had
> committed to paper.[9]

From her earliest years inventiveness was a compulsion, an
instinctive force which could not be denied, but by 1773 her
talents were harnessed transcribing work for her father's
General History of Music, a massive undertaking which
occupied them both many hours each day. Despite this
arduous commitment, she still found that her own creative
writing was vital to safeguard her own identity and in her
spare time she worked furiously on her journals, letters and
the imaginary correspondence which was to form her first
published novel, *Evelina*. Secrecy was an essential
ingredient. Cherishing the privacy of her unrestrained
thoughts, 'having my own way in total secrecy and silence to
all the world' was her one luxury. Yet it was a guilty pleasure
which had to be reserved for the afternoons and early hours of
the morning, when no-one could justifiably accuse her of
neglecting family duties. So careful was she that when
Evelina was eventually published anonymously even
members of her own family did not discover the true author
until months after the book's appearance.

Written in the scraps of time saved from other tasks,

Evelina appeared in 1778 and was an overwhelming success. The novel's format – letters sent from a young girl in London to an elderly gentleman in the country – clearly owed a great deal to Fanny's own correspondence with Mr Crisp. Evelina herself, in many ways a projection of Burney's own Cinderella fantasies, caught the public imagination with her freshness of perception and her unerring comic sense. The novel ran into four editions before the end of the following year and, when the author's identity became known, the spread of fame produced typically conflicting reactions in her. 'Indeed', she wrote, having retreated to Mr Crisp's country home for safety, 'in the midst of the greatest satisfaction that I feel, an inward something which I cannot account for, prepares me to expect a reverse; for the more the book is drawn into notice the more exposed it becomes to criticism and remark.' Nevertheless, she could not hide for ever and despite her trepidation she accepted an invitation to meet the formidable Mrs Thrale, who was longing to be introduced to the sharp mind that had produced *Evelina*.

Hester Lynch Thrale, a noted wit and fashionable hostess, drew Fanny into a charmed circle of literary elite, at the centre of which was the great Dr Johnson. Flattered, Burney responded wholeheartedly to their attentions, ignoring warnings from Mr Crisp who anticipated dangers in being beguiled by such appealing patronage. He advised her against their possible damaging influence on any work in progress. 'Let it be all your own till it is finished in entirely your own way', he recommended, for 'in these cases generally the more cooks, the worse broth'. Yet Fanny warmed to the encouragement of her new friends and their praise of her dramatic gifts, pressingly endorsed by Richard Brinsley Sheridan and Sir Joshua Reynolds, inspired her to start on a play. *The Witlings* was completed in 1779, a biting satiric comedy, attacking, rather to Mrs Thrale's surprise, the pretensions of scholarly women. Ironically, the most obstructive criticism came not from the Johnson coterie but from Mr Crisp himself and her father and it was criticism which was to have a lasting effect on Burney's literary career. Disregarding any merits the play might have, they demanded that she suppress it entirely, objecting to its topical content and to its ruthless lampooning style, which they feared would rapidly destroy her image of womanly modesty and gentleness. Severely shaken, she obeyed their wishes. 'Upon your account any disgrace would mortify and afflict me more than upon my own', she wrote meekly to her father, 'for whatever appears with your knowledge will naturally be supposed to have met with your approbation.' The pressure of her position as dutiful daughter gradually reasserted itself as Fanny bowed to Dr Burney's wishes and began work in the mode considered now most suitable by her superiors, another novel.

The composition of *Cecilia*, begun during 1780, soon became for her an arduous activity. Desperately trying to satisfy the expectations of her two taskmasters as well as a reading public who were all agog for a new work from the authoress of *Evelina*, Fanny Burney felt bitterly that she was no longer her own mistress. Writing had become not a secret indulgence but a chore which had to measure up to the exacting standards of a critical audience. Much of her spontaneity was crushed as she attempted to apply her talents to an uncongenial literary task and she became ill with the effort of trying to please. 'I am afraid of seeing my father', she confessed to her sister Susan. 'He will expect me to have just done when I am so behindhand as not even to see land'. Worrying and planning, she lay awake at night, and writing frenziedly, exhausted herself by day. At last, the first draft was finished but before she had time to revise it properly the manuscript was rushed to the press. Much to her chagrin, the booksellers had advertised *Cecilia* before Fanny had written the ending but in spite of the hurried circumstances of its production, the book was an enormous success. Much longer than *Evelina*, it contained the same magical combination of satiric realism and romantic fantasy and the first edition sold out almost at once. The book became the talk of fashionable London, people claiming that they had read it three times in succession, yet Fanny had still not acclimatised herself to mass adulation. Dreading being labelled 'clever' or of being associated with that notorious group of scholarly women, the *bas bleus*, she shrank from public notice and clung fiercely to the childlike image she had always cultivated. Dr Johnson often referred to her as the 'little Burney'; Daddy Crisp addressed her still as 'Fannikins' and admirers who met her for the first time were amazed to discover a retiring girl instead of the incisive, acerbic wit they expected. Even when she was nearing middle age, it was remarked by Mme de Staël that she still behaved like a schoolgirl of fourteen! This was Fanny Burney's safeguard. The exterior of adolescence provided her with a protective mechanism, a clearly defined role behind which she could conceal her inner self and which she knew she could rely on to retain the love and protection of her father and Mr Crisp. The act of writing which had originally seemed such a liberating force, had unwittingly turned into a weapon of what she feared most, exposure.

Submissiveness too contained its own dangers and, when in 1786 Fanny Burney was offered a position at Court as Second Keeper of the Robes to Queen Charlotte, she accepted, despite her natural aversion to the idea. Royalty held no glamour for her and she cared nothing for prestige but her father's obvious delight at the opportunity subdued her protests. Reluctantly she acquiesced, guessing only something of the horrors the new life had in store for her. Previously unwilling to lose her liberty through marriage, she was to find herself more restricted in the five years at court than she would have been with any husband. Her life at Windsor and Kew was repressive and composed of almost unalleviated boredom, with little time she could call her own. She was officially on duty from approximately seven in the morning until midnight or even later, many of those hours

Gramley Library
Salem College
Winston-Salem, NC 27108

spent patiently waiting for her Royal mistress or handling her
cumbersome and elaborate gowns. An added irony was her
indifference to dress. Fashion, like many another
conventional attribute, interested her only as a target for
burlesque. But her new life demanded meticulous attention
to details of her own costume as well as the Queen's, for she
had to appear appropriately garbed for all occasions. Queen
Charlotte, although Burney came to adore her, proved an
inconsiderate mistress, oblivious to the fatigue of her
attendants standing for hours behind her chair or outside her
door. Isolated from her family and separated from her
friends, Fanny had to suffer too the tyrannies of the vicious
Mrs Schwellenberg, an overbearing German who was her
immediate superior and who jealously guarded her rank by
humiliating Fanny or sabotaging her privacy.

Although there were occasional respites, such as her
presence as observer at the trial of Warren Hastings, the
Governor General of India who was impeached for
corruption, the pattern of Fanny's days was characterised by
tedium, exhaustion and degradation. Apart from her
preciously defended journal, her only means of psychological
release, her writing was limited to some morose verse
tragedies, influenced by her desolate environment. In 1791,
after nearly five years of subordinating her own impulses and
feelings, Fanny Burney could stand no more. Never strong in
health, she was becoming positively ill with the physical and
emotional hardships of court routine. She begged to be
allowed to resign her post but the Queen was slow to
appreciate her difficulties. In a heart-rending letter to her
family, Burney described how 'though I was so frequently ill
in her presence that I could hardly stand, I saw she concluded
me, while life remained, inevitably hers'. It was not for
several months that she was released from this slavery and
allowed to return home but her experience had changed her.
The natural gaiety of her temperament had been repressed
by the rigours of enforced obedience and incessant

formality and the introspective years spent starved of mental stimulation had fundamentally altered her attitude to life.

A source of emotional satisfaction appeared when Fanny met M. Alexandre D'Arblay, a gentle and cultured French refugee, while staying with her sister Susan in Surrey. Burney's perspective on the French Revolution, coloured by a daily association with a small group of shocked and charming émigrés, was radically different from the idealistic fervour of Romantic enthusiasts. Because of her own closeness to Royal family life, the execution of Louis XVI affected her deeply and her growing intimacy with these exiles engendered her sympathy with their sufferings at seeing their world devastated. She responded to their ability to adapt to new circumstances, their enthusiasm for life, their sparkle and wit in the face of potential hopelessness. D'Arblay, who added personal and military distinction to these qualities, was a magnetic character and Fanny found him totally irresistible. If she remembered her comments to Mrs Thrale ten years before, she carefully distinguished now between her own circumstances and those of her former friend. Her father, predictably, took a hostile view of the proposed match between a middle-aged spinster and a penniless refugee. He was assiduous in trying to dissuade her from an imprudent attachment but Fanny, in love for the first time with a man her own age and perhaps increasingly sensitive to the disastrous effects of her father's past advice, ignored him and married D'Arblay in July 1793. For some months they lived blissfully in Surrey. Their son, Alex, born the following year, added to their personal happiness but, as they were dependent on Fanny's court pension of £100 per year, their financial situation was precarious and they recognised that only her writing could rescue them from near penury. A calamitous performance of her verse tragedy, *Edwy and Elgiva*, at Drury Lane, which was greeted by an 'angelic' audience who 'only laughed when it was *impossible* to avoid it',[10] convinced her that another novel was their only recourse and accordingly she began work on *Camilla*.

Burney had lost none of her inventiveness or her dramatic power – the sustained vividness of her journals proves that – but writing for a market was quite different from scribbling for her own enjoyment. Her perspective too had changed. She was no longer young and the idea of *A Picture of Youth*, as *Camilla* was subtitled, suggested a moral seriousness which she felt now incumbent upon her. As breadwinner, a strange reversal of roles had taken place and she resolved to adapt to her new responsibilities and the new awareness of self which her marriage had affected. Dominated by economic concerns, she decided to bring out *Camilla* by subscription and requested permission to dedicate it to the Queen. The whole method of production smacked of its public nature and to emphasise its edifying character Burney insisted on calling it a 'work' rather than a 'novel'. Based on memories of her own family in childhood, the book dealt directly with matters of conduct but its overtly didactic tone stifled the dramatic liveliness that had been shown in the realisation of similar issues in *Evelina* and *Cecilia*. Burney's attempt to please all sections of her audience was seriously miscalculated and drew unfavourable reviews. 'There was but one opinion about it' ruefully quoted her brother, Charles. 'Mme D'Arblay was determined to fill 5 volumes – and had done it in such a manner as would do her no credit.' As some consolation, he wrote his sister a cheering message:

'Now heed no more what critics thought 'em
Since this you know – All People bought 'em'.

And indeed *Camilla*, published in 1796, was to be the most financially rewarding of all her books and the D'Arblays were able to buy their own home on the proceeds.

During the next few years, Fanny produced some of her best, although some of her least known, works – comedies for the stage. These scintillating plays, *Love and Fashion*, *The Woman Hater* and *A Busy Day*, demonstrate the flowering of the theatrical talent that the Thrale circle had detected in her so many years before. Written while she was unencumbered by family demands or onerous social duties, they provide further insights into Burney's creative mainsprings. Her inner life, fecund as ever, could operate freely only when outside pressures were removed. Painfully self analytical and obsessed with notions of duty, her works deal constantly with the difficulties of adapting the private life to social forms and her own creative process itself expresses many of these difficulties. Her career emerges as a story of compromise as she fluctuated between the joy in giving her thoughts free reign and the determination to meet what she felt others required.

In 1801, M. D'Arblay returned to France to try to recover his property and re-establish his position there. He was given a ministry post and later joined the French Royalist Guard and fought at Waterloo. The conflict between Fanny's two identities, as woman and as writer, was again at work when in 1802 she went to join her husband and her plays were never performed. Once more she devoted her life to domestic concerns, prevented by the onset of war from getting back to England. It was ten years before she saw her father again and throughout that period she worked sporadically on her fourth novel, a lengthy account of a young woman's attempt to earn her own living in a friendless and alien society. Back in England in 1812, she luxuriated in the joys of reunion. Alex, who was now at Cambridge, was busily incurring expenses for his mother that she found difficult to meet and she decided to complete the manuscript of *The Wanderer* in order to support them. 'Tired am I of my pen! Oh tired! tired!' she moaned to Charles as she toiled away laboriously. Her name alone was sufficient to sell the work which appeared in 1814 to eager public anticipation. Once more, however, she had misjudged her market. Perhaps her long absence from the literary scene had blinkered her to recent trends, in particular the increased prestige of novels. No longer a genre to be ashamed of, or to be hurriedly burnt on a bonfire in case of discovery, fiction had acquired a respectability that made Mme D'Arblay's introductory apology for her novel almost embarrassing and its critical reception was dispiriting. *The Wanderer*, however, with its focus on women's isolation and suffering, articulates many of the tensions that had informed Burney's own experience. In part too it can be seen as her response to the aggressive feminist pamphlets which had provoked the current interest in the 'woman question'. Its technique, however, creaked.

The Wanderer was Burney's last fictional work, although until her death in 1840 she continued to produce journals and letters as vivid as any of her earlier writings, if often more sombre in tone. Her account of her horrific operation for breast cancer, undertaken without anaesthetic, and her description of her husband's last illness are totally compelling in their immediacy and power. Yet Burney's published work frequently falls short of the highest standards of which she was capable. When almost eighty, she began her last project, editing her late father's hoard of miscellaneous documents and trying scrupulously to structure them into an ordered memoir. It was published in 1832 to derisive reviews but Fanny had not felt able to trust anyone else with the enterprise. In spite of being such a practised writer she was still capable of gross errors of judgement and inconsistencies of style. The question of this discrepancy between her private and public writings is one of the most puzzling aspects of her career, an aspect reflected in the many contradictions of her life. Her personal courage suprisingly often defied the forms of femininity that she appeared to find so intimidating. In 1815 for instance she left Paris and undertook a six-day, ghastly journey to Brussels to find her husband at the battle of Waterloo. It was hardly the sort of journey one would expect a demure and proper lady to make without protection, along roads dense with vagrants and starving and desperate soldiers, but Burney did not consider courage necessarily incompatible with propriety. In her quiet way she was always prepared to defy those conventions that interfered with her primary allegiances and her outward orthodoxy concealed a revolutionary spirit which always emerged in her novels however much she attempted to muffle it.

Fanny Burney's long life spanned a period of immense change in attitudes to women. She was born into a world of unchallenged male supremacy, a world where women, if they spoke at all, spoke largely as they had been taught – with the voices of men. By the time she was old, a distinctively female voice had emerged, a voice that told repeatedly of suffering, silence and peremptory obedience to the will of others, a voice too that suggested strategies of survival. Burney contributed centrally to that voice and it was no accident that this transition coincided with the upsurge of the novel and its expanding hold in the minds of women, both as readers and practitioners.

What was the appeal of fiction to eighteenth-century women? Certainly, early novels catered for the demands of the new female reading public. Their subjects dealt with the fabric of feminine lives, domestic details, questions of conduct, debates about social morality, issues that were crucially relevant to a newly cultivated bourgeoisie seeking self-definition. The romantic bias of fiction not only satisfied women's fantasies, which were often thwarted by the social realities they encountered, but vindicated the importance of the inner life to a section of the population who, prevented from entering the outer world of commerce or the professions, were thrown on the resources of their emotions. As Jane Austen's Anne Elliot in *Persuasion*, was to explain, 'We live at home, quiet, confined, and our feelings prey upon us'.[11] Partly as a result of such enforced solitude, women became active correspondents. Diaries and letters were used as emotional outlets and helped to define and sharpen the reality of daily life. It was only natural therefore that autobiographical and epistolary forms should provide the narrative direction for much early fiction.

It has been estimated that the years 1770–90 saw literacy increase fourfold, so when circulating libraries, whose stock consisted almost entirely of novels, began lending volumes for as little as twopence each, the consumer market for fiction rapidly expanded. At the same time, women saw economic and creative possibilities in novel writing. Novels seemed a natural extension of the talents utilised in personal journals and did not rely on an esoteric scholarly tradition from which women with their more mundane educational backgrounds were excluded. It seemed easy to write novels. Their relative accessibility and the vast rate of production towards the turn of the century meant inevitably that most novels were intellectually lightweight, intended for a largely un-discriminating public, and it was generally believed that the form, having peaked with the work of Richardson and Fielding, was now on its way out. Undeniably, many of the contents of lending libraries were exotic romances or fictional 'memoirs', which abounded with scenes of abduction, rape, incest, false marriages, betrayals, murder, suicide and a whole range of ingeniously gory deaths. It was not surprising that novels were considered shocking, suitable only for the most frivolous minds, encouraging a view of women as an inferior species, lacking mental and moral fibre. As a critic of 1770 postulated about novel readers, 'A large majority, especially of the fair sex, have not time nor talents for the investigation of abstract principles, in moral and social life, wherefore a lighter kind of study is essential'.[12] It was assumed accordingly that novel writing required little ability and was the result of an overactive imagination fantasising on improper subjects. No wonder that Burney, brought up in a household of intellectuals, at the age of fifteen equated fiction with 'degradation' and felt guiltily compelled to destroy her own compositions.

Women's autobiographies, such as Charlotte Charke's in 1755, only reinforced the disreputable status of women's writing. In sensationalising the events of her life, Mrs Charke projected a public identity akin to the most reprobate fictional character: aggressive, violent, egoistic and sexually outrageous. She dressed in men's clothes and proposed 'marriage' to a young lady of fortune. Writers of fiction too were considered immoral. Eliza Haywood, victim of an unhappy marriage, tried to support herself and her two children by writing, first for the stage, then with a series of romances and finally with two novels, *The History of Miss Betsey Thoughtless* (1751) and *The History of Jemmy and Jenny Jessamy* (1753), both of which, in enquiring into the values of marriage, portrayed independent-minded women. The author's own unconventional personal life was sufficient condemnation for both her and her books and, rather unfairly, her children were automatically assumed to be illegitimate. Similarly, Elizabeth Inchbald, actress turned author, was widely believed to lead an immoral life although there was no evidence to support imputations of lewdness, and her best work, *A Simple Story*, criticised her high-spirited heroine for overstepping the limits of feminine modesty. To remain respectable, respectable women needed to retain their privacy. The stigma of unchastity that clung to early women writers was not necessarily based on scandalous events in their lives or in their writing but was a corollary of self-exposure, at odds with the contemporary code of female reticence.

Consequently, many women published anonymously, rather than risk their personal reputations. Or they apologised profusely for their work, excusing it by pleading extreme financial pressure or by justifying it through its unimpeachable moral nature and didactic value. Sarah

Fielding's dedication to *The Governess* in 1749 was typical.

> The design of the following sheets is to endeavour to
> cultivate an early inclination to Benevolence, and a love of
> Virtue in the minds of young women, by trying to shew
> them that their true interest is concerned in cherishing and
> improving those amiable dispositions into Habits, and
> in keeping down all those rough and boisterous
> Passions. . . . This I have endeavoured to inculcate, by
> those methods of Fable and Moral.[13]

Perhaps the key word here is 'interest', as Miss Fielding
acknowledges that women must cultivate the pleasing arts
and must suppress any inclinations that might prejudice their
chances in the sexual market. Didacticism was acceptable as
a pretext for female novelists, whose writing was placed in a
separate category by male critics and treated with patronising
tolerance – bad grammar and poor spelling being benignly
disregarded. The worst fault was seen as intellectual
pretension and women struggled to convince readers of their
own gaucherie. 'A candid, a liberal, a generous Public, will
make the necessary allowances for the *first* attempt of a young
female Adventurer in Letters', coyly pleaded one authoress,
who firmly repudiated any suggestion that her book might be
'deserving of the approbation of the judicious'.[14] Everything
bore witness to that incompatibility between the roles of
writer and conventional femininity that Burney's work
articulates so tellingly.

The character of women's fiction was not uniformly
deferential despite the apologies with which it was often
accompanied. As the patterns of women's experience began
to emerge, so did individual heroines who questioned the
accepted definitions of female passivity. Mrs Inchbald's Miss
Milner in *A Simple Story* indicates the impact of passion as an
undeniable force and her rebelliousness, although punished
in the novel, remains its dominant and its most attractive

feature. Women were prepared too to satirise men's attempts to control their development, as in Charlotte Smith's delightfully tongue in cheek *Emmeline* (1788).

> He protested too against Emmeline for affecting knowledge – 'It is', said he, 'a maxim of my father's – and my father is no bad judge – that for a woman to affect literature is the most horrid of all absurdities; and for a woman to know anything of business is detestable!' Mrs. Ashwood laid by her dictionary, determined for the future to spell her own way without it.[15]

Women were beginning to fight back against their categorisation as submissive simpletons, both in fiction and in the polemical statements which presented more directly the case for female emancipation. Mary Wollstonecraft's *A Vindication of the Rights of Women* (1792) argued vehemently against sexual stereotyping. 'I do earnestly wish to see the distinction of sex confounded in society', she declared, 'for this distinction is, I am firmly persuaded, the foundation of the weakness of character ascribed to women.[16] In insisting on equality and women's potential for action and independence, she emphasised the importance of education in determining self awareness, stressing the innate rationality of women's minds. Nor was hers a lone voice. Mary Hays, a friend of Wollstonecraft, and like her a lifelong campaigner for women's rights, published *An Appeal to the Men of Great Britain on Behalf of the Women* (1798). Both Hays and Priscilla Wakefield, whose *Reflections on the Present Condition of the Female Sex* appeared in the same year, challenged male assumptions about women's roles and their expectations of compliance and obedience. Their work had a clear political bias, as they demanded that women be allowed to contribute to the economic value of their society, instead of being dismissed as useless adornments. The case was pushed even further by Mary Ann Radcliffe who, in her own search for

gainful employment, could discover no occupation available
to women except prostitution. Her *The Female Advocate; or
an Attempt to Recover the Rights of Women from Male
Usurpation* (1799) described the condition of prostitutes and
put the blame for their plight squarely on public indifference
to the question of women's poverty.

These women in their fight for freedom provoked a storm
of conservative reaction. The manner of their protest as well
as its matter incited furious resistance from an audience alive
to the threat of insurrection and a spate of counter arguments
began to appear. 'I am sure I have as much liberty as I can
make use of, now I am an old maid; and when I was a young
girl, I had, I dare say, more than was good for me',
maintained Hannah More waspishly. 'To be unstable and
capricious . . . is but too characteristic of our sex; and there is
perhaps no animal so much indebted to subordination for its
good behaviour as woman.'[17] Caught up in this climate of
incertitude were many, like Fanny Burney, whose stand was
ambivalent. The woman's novel had always shown itself
sensitive to the very issues now publicised by the
controversy. Many women were aware of the restrictive
nature of their lives, while simultaneously recognising their
own vulnerability in a social system controlled by male power
and the dangers thus inherent in revolutionary change.
Quietly, women had been developing literary methods for
exposing the iniquities of the system and for creating a forum
for their views. Whereas fiction provided scope for a degree
of subtlety in the expression of subversive attitudes, the
propagandist work of Wollstonecraft and others involved
tactics that seemed doomed to failure in a climate so hostile to
extremism. In addition, militancy was directly in conflict
with many women's interests, economically dependent as
they were on masculine support.

For Fanny Burney, all her life dominated by fear of male
authority, the current schism held particular poignancy. In
many ways it gave voice to the perennial confusions which

informed her own sense of identity and her writing. When in her journal, she confessed, 'I would a thousand times rather forfeit my character as a writer than risk ridicule or censure as a female', the personal dilemma she describes embodied the perplexities of the age.

2 Fanny Burney's Heroines

The two modes of writing that Burney principally employed seem to reflect the separate worlds that she inhabited, the public and the private. Whereas her journals are unrestrained and direct – they confront emotion without melodrama and their style is fresh and effortless – her novels, reliant on conventions, are deeply indebted to contemporary literary models. Such disparity of method endorses the idea of the tensions of personality that Fanny Burney experienced, her struggle to blend self and society, and it is a struggle that all her writing in some way affirms.

The novels share a common theme, a theme which was to become increasingly familiar to readers of nineteenth-century fiction. It is identified in the subtitle to *Evelina – A Young Lady's Entrance into the World* – and was a subject of fundamental importance to eighteenth-century women, whose situation and status was in the process of being reassessed and debated. The theme of the ingenue's first encounter with society was not in itself a female prerogative. Fielding's Tom Jones was perhaps the most influential of the literary innocents whose values, in many ways superior to those of his fellows, must yet be tempered by prudence before he could become fully integrated. Samuel Richardson's Clarissa had become an archetypal figure of female victimisation, suffering at the hands of an unscrupulous and powerful male aggressor. The impact of this legacy on Fanny Burney cannot be overestimated. For by the late eighteenth century, the topic of social initiation had acquired a special relevance for women and was put to particular use by Burney, who probed so searchingly the uncertainties and anomalies of a woman's position in a man's world. Each of her novels contains a study of an adolescent heroine and progressively charts stages in her efforts to gain social recognition, beginning with Evelina's naivety as she tentatively negotiates metropolitan values on her first visit to London. This variant on the favourite eighteenth-century theme of the opposition between nature and art was developed by Fanny Burney so as to have specific implications for women, perplexed as they were about their social roles. For, like Cecilia and Juliet in *The Wanderer*, Evelina is a girl without parental support, unprotected in a powerful and exclusive society. How can she best survive? That is the question posed by all the novels, as Burney's heroines try to adapt their own intuitive sense of value to the practical demands of existence that confront them.

All Burney's heroines are alone. All journey away from a secure base into unknown territory. This movement, so popular in eighteenth-century fiction, of a journey away from a father's house, reflects in Burney's novels a metaphorical estrangement from familiar and supportive values. Evelina keeps in touch with her moral centre via her letters to her safe and reliable guardian, the Rev. Mr Villars, but Cecilia, Burney's second heroine, has no such prop. All apparent sources of support are one by one removed from her and, as her guardians prove successively unreliable, she is forced back on her own judgement, facing the undeniable fact of her own isolation. In the third novel, Camilla, unlike the other heroines, is provided with a family but in becoming separated from them she too becomes the victim of misunderstandings. When familial sympathy is removed she stands to lose everything. The later novels' departure from the spontaneous personal narrative of *Evelina* is accompanied by a progressively darkening vision, as the dangers resulting from social rejection are made ferociously explicit. The melodramatic fates of the heroines, however, have their parallels in actual social documentation and historical fact. Destitution, imprisonment, incarceration in a lunatic asylum were all real possibilities for women who strayed from the path of virtue. In *The Wanderer*, the portrayal of Juliet, the fair Incognita, expands this sense of victimisation. Through her disguise and her refusal to give her real name, attention is forced on her representative function and, as the threats magnify, the real instability of women's social identity is disclosed.

Clearly, the continuing dialogue about women's position in contemporary society is mirrored in these novels, which articulate the central issues of the controversy. The works after *Evelina*, in particular, demonstrate an awareness of the problematic nature of women's roles. Burney's heroines do not exist solely in domestic situations but are presented always in a wider social context. They are never seen as wives and mothers (although Camilla's filial duties are sternly put to the test) but as potentially independent beings. Burney is concerned with problems of inheritance and questions of economics. She agonises over Cecilia's fortune and her helplessness in the face of unscrupulous men determined to defraud her. Her other heiress, Eugenia Tyrold, is shown as dreadfully at risk because she is quite unaware of the value of the money which turns her into a marketable object. In the same book, Camilla's financial ignorance is used to demonstrate the evils of gambling and the desperate consequences of debt. Money is the hallmark of Fanny Burney's society and women are shown to be woefully inadequate in handling it. The growth of the commercial society had given middle-class women leisure and respectability which ironically removed them from the source of the activity which shaped their position. Anticipating this situation, Defoe, half a century earlier, had complained that certain trades were becoming not 'proper' for women, 'such as linen and woollen drapers, mercers and goldsmiths, all sorts of dealers by commission and the like. Custom I say, has made these trades so effectually to shut out the women, that what with custom and the women's generally thinking it below them, we never or rarely see any women in such shops and warehouses.'[1]

This gradual exclusion of women from the commercial world resulted naturally in their increased ignorance of business matters and their consequent helplessness and dependence on men. At the time of writing *Camilla*, Fanny Burney was herself peculiarly alert to the problems of earning a living. Marriage to D'Arblay, an unemployed, impecunious foreigner, meant that she was the one now responsible for supporting her family. From this unusual viewpoint, she was able to visualise without sentimentality the limitations of education in equipping girls to deal with the harsh realities of economic existence. *The Wanderer* of course clarifies and intensifies the nature of this problem as Juliet acknowledges the difficulties of finding employment.

> 'How few', she cried, 'how circumscribed are the attainments of women! and how much fewer and more circumscribed still are those which may, in their consequences, be useful as well as ornamental to the higher or educated!'

Juliet is required to perform a delicate balancing act. She must ward off starvation while still maintaining her respectability. Her gentility is one potential avenue to eventual social acceptance and she has to be careful not to compromise it. She learns bitterly not only the inadequacy of her own skills but also how few are 'those through which, in the reverses of fortune, a FEMALE may reap benefit without abasement!'

All Fanny Burney's heroines find themselves in precarious positions and have to tread warily over the abyss of social disapproval in order to secure the rich husband who will give

them a name and protection. In Burney's world, no other
realistic solution can guarantee both freedom of movement
and dinner on the table. Without society, Fanny Burney's
women have no identity; society is the all-powerful authority
which can make or break their futures. Social errors form the
main sources of fear for her heroines. Recognising the weight
carried by social codes, Burney portrays her upper-class
English communities as if they are alien tribes, with strange
rituals which have to be learned by the initiate before full
acceptance can take place.

If the emphasis in the novels on problems of courtesy
seems trivial to our twentieth-century consciousness, we
must remember that for Fanny Burney and her heroines,
etiquette was the only currency available. Her interest in
manners is by no means frivolous but part of a deep
understanding of the social mechanisms that exert such
influence in shaping the lives of individuals. The warning of
Evelina's serious-minded clergyman, Mr Villars, that
'nothing is so delicate as the reputation of a woman; it is at
once the most beautiful and most brittle of all human things',
relates crucially to Burney's perception of social and sexual
roles, and her understanding of women's essential
vulnerability. Evelina's faux pas at the ball, for instance,
when she refuses one partner and then accepts another,
exposes a complicated network of male–female relationships
and their far-reaching political effects.

In stressing the importance of conduct, Fanny Burney
reflects one of the major preoccupations of her age. From the
beginning of the century, essays on social behaviour had
appeared in the pages of *The Tatler* and *The Spectator*, the
latter advertising itself as a 'work which endeavours to
cultivate and polish human life', and both periodicals
illustrating the contemporary interest in the relationship
between manners and morals. The self-consciousness of the
newly educated middle class and its need for confidence-
strengthening is evident not only in the witty pamphleteering

of Addison and Steele, and later in Johnson's *The Rambler* and *The Idler*, but also in the plethora of courtesy books, aimed particularly at women, that began to appear as the century wore on. Dr Fordyce's *Sermons to Young Women*, which was first published in 1765, was still thought worthy when Jane Austen described Lydia Bennet's truculent reaction to its moralistic tedium thirty years later. Almost as enduring were Mrs Chapone's *Essays on the Improvement of the Mind* (1772) and Dr Gregory's *A Father's Legacy to His Daughters* (1774). These, together with a spate of lesser known works, combined religious precepts with detailed advice on domestic conduct and were highly recommended for their improving educational value. Girls were taught to avoid coquetry and artifice and instead to cultivate the virtues of modesty, obedience and (significantly) silence, for 'a very young woman can hardly be too silent and reserved in company.'[2] They were advised on dress, on deportment and on which accomplishments were considered suitable. Behaviour was seen as an accurate indicator of ethical principles. 'Modesty and unassuming carriage in people of talent and fame, are irresistible', wrote Fanny Burney to Mr Crisp after one evening party. 'How much do I prefer for acquaintance the well-bred and obliging Miss Davies to the self-sufficient and imperious Bastardini, though I doubt not the superiority of her powers as a singer.' And she was later to condemn the apparently worthy Mr Barlow who applied for her hand because he had 'no elegance of manners'.

Gradually conduct books attempted to enliven their sermonising with brief illustrative narratives and, as fiction increased its appeal, a series of novels were produced with overt didactic messages. As J. M. S. Tompkins has pointed out, the titles alone are sufficient to announce the motives of books such as *The Exemplary Mother* (1769), *Victim of Fancy* (1787) and *The School for Widows* (1791), which trailed in the wake of the courtesy book wave. Time and again minor novels of the period such as these portrayed the model young lady, an assiduous pupil of Dr Fordyce and his followers, artless, elegant and submissive. Burney's heroines similarly indicate their origins. Evelina, Cecilia, Camilla and Juliet are all innocents, untainted by show or forward behaviour. Their natural impulses inspire modesty: they cast their eyes downward: they do not gaze boldly: they blush easily. But one of Burney's greatest achievements was that she was able to manipulate these conventions for her own ends and to transcend the formulae that she also exploited.

In probing the intricate relationship between self and society, Fanny Burney equips her women with many of the characteristics of sentimental fiction. Sentimentalism, the cult of sensibility, had arisen in mid-century as a result of the expanding interest in the values of personal experience. In an age when the court itself was becoming increasingly domesticated (Burney's diary shows us a king who drinks barley-water after hunting, a queen who does embroidery and a princess who gets 'the snuffles') Burney's novels depict accurately the shift of emphasis from thinking big to thinking small. Her heroines have to ensure social acceptance it is true but the society she envisages is one composed of family gatherings, shopping, evening parties and theatre visits. Her characters spend much of their time reading, drawing, sewing and going for walks. Her social politics focus on the dynamics of personal relationships.

For the true sentimentalist, the quality of life was observed to reside in trivial occasions and the mind capable of appreciating the finer details of experience was thought of as possessing a degree of sophistication beyond the vulgarian's reach. To be responsive to the delicacy of momentary sensations, to recognise the significance of the casual glance, touch or minute, was to realise in oneself the true refinements of sensibility. In Mary Wollstonecraft's words sensibility was 'the most exquisite feeling of which the human soul is capable, . . . acute senses, finely fashioned nerves which vibrate at the slightest touch, and convey such clear intelligence to the brain that it does not require to be arranged by the judgement'.[3] Such extreme sensitivity became endowed with moral properties, as the feeling heart was seen as a reliable guide for action. Compassion and benevolence for those less fortunate than oneself were emotions engendered by the extension of the bonds of human sympathy. Evelina's pity for the desolate Mr Macartney is aroused by a chance encounter as they pass one another on the stairs. She is attracted by his air of melancholy, an obvious give-away to his own highly developed sensibility, and by the notion that she might be able to relieve his sufferings. But benevolence remained in the eighteenth century a private action, capable of giving as much satisfaction to the donor as to the recipient, and in *Evelina* her charitable impulses are an illustration of the heroine's own sensitivity as much as anything else.

All Burney's young women are emotionally responsive, highly susceptible to trivial stimuli and easily moved. Their tears flow but Burney makes sure that they flow only with good cause. She was particularly scathing about the excesses of sentimentalism. When one evening in company at Mrs Thrale's she met the beautiful Sophy Streatfield, who wept on request to demonstrate her extreme tenderness of heart, she records how 'two crystal tears came into the soft eyes of the S.S. and rolled gently down her cheeks! Such a sight I never saw before, nor could I have believed. She offered not to conceal or dissipate them; on the contrary she really contrived to have them seen by everybody . . . . Loud and rude bursts of laughter broke from us all at once. How indeed could they be restrained?' There is for Burney a sharp distinction to be drawn between the melting, instinctive response of the genuinely soft heart and the deliberate cultivation of its more showy effects. So although her heroines weep easily there is always proper occasion and while they incorporate many of the stereotypic features of other literary models, Burney is insistent on their capacity for rational thought.

It is judgement which operates in Evelina's and Cecilia's censure of the attitudes of polite society. They are critical of foppishness, of extravagant behaviour and of slavish followers of fashion. Cecilia receives cynically her instructions on how to converse in the approved mode. 'So much', she chaffs her tutor, 'for sorrow and for affectation. Proceed next to stupidity; for that in all probability, I shall most frequently encounter.' And Evelina can 'scarce forbear laughing' when asked to dance by a young man whose fashionable behaviour seems to her only outlandish and affected. As well as independent thought, these women are also quite capable of independent action. Evelina, for instance, has no hesitation in snatching at loaded pistols, when there is no strong man around to tell her not to. The sensibility of Burney's heroines is always carefully balanced by an active intelligence. The heart and the head combine in their portrayal.

Fanny Burney was a realist. Her attitude towards the literary clichés she employs is sceptical and her novels easily assimilate the melodramatic elements into the overall comic scenario. Her plots for instance incorporate many of the features of conventional romance. *Evelina* and *Camilla* are merely versions of the Cinderella theme, a staple ingredient of eighteenth-century novels since Richardson's brilliant adaptaton of it in *Pamela*. The story of the Princess and the Pea, gentility in rags, is retold through the experiences of Cecilia and Juliet, the discovery of their true identity allowable only after a series of tests and a highly prolonged and extravagant denouement. Characters are painfully rejected by their loved ones and then gloriously reunited. They are threatened with penury, starvation, madness, abduction and they encounter suicide attempts and deathbed scenes. The heroines marry elitist and aristocratic heroes, who frequently have little but their station in life to recommend them. Yet although the narrative direction of her novels follows these well tried formulae, Burney's main interest is not in the contrivances of the plot nor in romance but in the social comedy and its illumination of individual dilemmas.

It is not the action but the heroine's response to the action which is foregrounded. Like their sentimental predecessors, the characters are confronted with experience that they cannot immediately control. Their social circumstances, where they live, whom they meet are all matters dictated for them, so that major choices are removed from them but their capacity for judgement is not. Thus it is the characters' minds which become the focus of interest and the quality of their experience which provides the narrative dynamic. This view of the mind as a sensitive receptacle which absorbed experience and responded accordingly was not in itself new. The sentimental emphasis on the values of individualism had produced a range of central characters who were required to make sense of the chaotic flux of experience which surrounded them – notably Sterne's Uncle Toby in *Tristram Shandy* and Yorick in *A Sentimental Journey* or the heroes of Henry Mackenzie. In these novels, coherent action reduced to a minimum, the sensations and intricacies of personality sustained the overall direction. Burney of course does not aspire to Sterne's literary or philosophical sophistication, nor does she wish to dispense in any way with the formal structures. The observance of the proprieties remained vital to her. She develops rather the interest in women's roles initially stimulated by Richardson, suggesting that the female mind is as worthy of attention as the male and that feminine experience has a unique dimension which justifies serious analysis. Less radical than Richardson, she has one advantage which was denied him: her own experience of growing up as a woman in a restrictive society. She seeks ways of best liberating the self and allowing the individual personality to find full expression without disturbing the social forms which necessarily provide constraints but which also provide structure.

In initiating what was to become the 'woman's novel' Fanny Burney adopts a mode which presents her readers with the very texture of women's lives and by so doing, establishes herself as a literary pioneer. William Hazlitt's comment that she 'is a quick, lively and accurate observer of persons and things' is sharpened by the recognition that 'she always looks at them with a consciousness of her sex, and in that point of view in which it is the particular business and interest of women to observe them'.[4] With no female vocabulary available to them previous women writers had fallen back on male techniques. Charlotte Charke, for instance, in her autobiography created a persona reminiscent of Defoe's Moll Flanders, a woman who could survive only by being like a man, adopting male disguise, travelling round the country, fighting and asserting her equality by partaking in traditionally male activities. Novelists, such as Eliza Haywood or Mary de la Rivière Manley, also employed a largely masculine tenor in recounting their histories. Action took precedence over character in their tales of adventure, fantastic exploits and broad panoramic scenes. The complexities of the personality were ignored, together with any idea of the shared and special nature of women's experience. But Fanny Burney discloses the essential fibre of women's daily lives as lives composed of trivia, where the choice of dress, the petty matters of conversation, the technicalities of hairdressing or reserving theatre seats are seen to carry significance. The extreme situations and creaking plot mechanisms are merely pegs on which to hang this material. Burney moves away from the episodic novels which preceded her to the coherence of *Evelina*, which uses the epistolary method so successfully employed by Richardson to blend thematic and narrative elements, and maintains the close focus on detailed experience which was to identify the common approach of so many later women novelists.

Apart from *Camilla*, Fanny Burney's novels are not conventionally didactic and even *Camilla* departs from its orthodox moralistic direction with a subtext which offers a challenge to certain prevailing standards. But Burney is deeply concerned with behavioural codes and in considering the nature of female lives her books illustrate a fundamentally prudential morality. Reworking her own experience through her novels, she demonstrates her own anxieties about doing the right thing and introduces a distinctively feminine perspective on the male hierarchy. Men appear as they impinge on women's experience. They are seen in their domestic roles, as fathers, brothers, potential husbands, all of whom can arbitrarily withhold love and deny support. They also appear as guardians, lawyers, bankers, the figureheads of officialdom with bureaucratic power. Frequently their roles overlap. The aristocratic Lord Orville represents for Evelina both the material security and social status that she craves and the love and moral constancy that will sustain her personal confidence. The power of masculine values is recognised and accepted, however inimical it might be to women's own sense of priorities.

As Patricia Meyer Spacks has observed,[5] Burney's women are dominated by a sense of fear, an emotion which shapes their attitudes and inspires their actions. The fear which projected itself in the Gothic novels of the period as deep-seated psychological phantasmagoria is transmuted in Burney's fiction into a setting of deceptively reassuring familiarity. The terror experienced by Burney's heroines is located in the minutiae of polite society. Evelina worries about her lack of polish and her vulgar relatives. Juliet is nervous about playing the harp in public. Camilla is distraught about her lover's discovery of innocently committed misdemeanours. Ignorance, exposure, mis-

interpretation – these are the anxieties that dog Burney's
women and reveal their fundamental confusion about how to
conduct themselves. 'I have been', cries Cecilia at a late stage
in the novel, 'too facile and too unguarded!' Despite her
original determination to 'think and live for herself', she is
forced to recognise the duplicity of her society and to learn
that she can never be fully independent of the community
which carries the power to destroy her. She is helpless in the
face of legal demands on her inheritance and defenceless in
the face of insidious rumours about her moral character.
Circumstances combine against her to initiate the cumulative
disasters of *Cecilia*'s final volume. In examining the problems
which beset social conformity, Burney's attitude is how can
women possibly survive in a society which is so obviously and
heavily weighted against them.

For Fanny Burney, women's social vulnerability is closely
associated with their sexual fragility. The novels are fraught
with sexual menace. The London of pleasure gardens and
bourgeois residential streets contains dangers as perilous and
as real as Mrs Radcliffe's wild foreign landscapes and isolated
castles with their antique chambers. Evelina's panic, lost in
the subliminally sinister dark alleys at Vauxhall dramatises
women's basic fear of personal violation. Evelina is 'terrified
to death', 'frightened exceedingly', 'distracted with terror'.
Attacked by a group of strange men who see her as legitimate
sexual game, she is rescued by another who, under the guise
of friendship, tries to seduce her and proves to be equally as
treacherous. It seems as if there is no escape. In stressing the
precariousness of the situation of the single woman, Burney
reveals that sexuality is an ambivalent attribute. It is both a
trap and a shield for the sex who can so easily be reduced to
gender characteristics. The veneer of polite society conceals
an atavistic violence against which women must constantly
be on their guard.

The dividing line between respectability and degradation
is always presented as a very narrow one. 'It is impossible and

improper to keep up acquaintance with a female who has lost her character, however sincerely she may be an object of pity', Burney noted in her diary of 1775, having just snubbed a rather shady young lady in the park. 'Much is to be said in excuse of a poor credulous young creature whose person is attractive while her mind is unformed' but there was no way that such sympathy could be corroborated by action. Burney was a creature of her time and her novels continually assert the tenuous nature of the hold women have on the world's approbation. Cecilia and Camilla are both mistaken for prostitutes when male protection is removed. Juliet and Cecilia are reluctantly inveigled into secret marriages against their better judgement. Confusion prevails. All these heroines are shrouded in mystery at some stage in their stories. Without men, their identity remains an enigma. The popular fictional motifs of unknown parentage, disguise, disinheritance and reconciliation are invested with a new dimension as Burney lays bare the problematics of self. Women's identity is seen as being reliant on male status but this in itself is shown as a hazardous source of refuge.

The burden of this examination of women's experience does not rest with the heroines alone. The novels contain a host of minor female characters who have independent contributions to make to the fabric of enquiry. All provide variants on the ideas of conformism and role-playing. Burney creates immature adolescents who marry without fully understanding what that means; she exposes the plight of old maids; she mocks girls who are over demonstrative and those who follow fashion unthinkingly; she ridicules women who are ignoramuses and women who are too educated for their own good; she paints women who are forceful and aggressive and women who attempt to live without male mentors. Her young lord who complains, 'I don't know what the devil a woman lives for after thirty; she is only in other folks' way', is a perfect prototype of male arrogance and an illustration of the tendency to classify women as dispensable items. Her heroines learn by bitter experience how to avoid this categorisation but Burney's lesser characters often indicate quite fully realised alternatives. They are not, as in many other contemporary novels, used merely as warning examples, foils for that moral paragon, the heroine, but are frequently presented with a degree of imaginative sympathy that intensifies the pattern of the whole.

This sympathy necessarily affects the portrayal of her male characters too. Much of Fanny Burney's critical reputation in the past has rested with these brilliantly vivid caricatures and satiric portraits but it is perhaps worthwhile noting that her men only seem to come alive when they are objects of attack. Her heroes are pale and uninteresting, spineless representatives of a dead value system. They engage her only as symbolic figures, providing the conventional disciplines of romance and moral authority which her lively heroines must ultimately acknowledge. Much of the time they are in fact absent from the narrative, remaining only in spirit as a guiding principle of the culture they embody, inspiring terror in the hearts of the heroines who seek their approval and directing their movements from a position offstage. But the clowns, fops, villains and fools have a stature and vitality that is instantly absorbing. Burney's comic sense, derived from the traditions of eighteenth-century satire, owes much to Fielding, Smollett and the Hogarthian tradition of the social cartoon. She scrutinises the details of manner and dress, notes the precision of idiomatic speech and the impact of visual idiosyncracies. These methods of observation were trained during her long apprenticeship to Mr Crisp, who demanded that her letters should provide him with a graphic reconstruction of events in London to enliven the solitude of his quiet country evenings. 'He is indeed very ill-favoured', begins her sharp dissection of Dr Johnson. 'Is tall and stout; but stoops terribly; he is almost bent double'. Each detail continues the process of devastation. 'His mouth is almost constantly opening and shutting, as if he was chewing. He has a strange method of frequently twirling his fingers, and twisting his hands. His body is in continual agitation, *see-sawing* up and down; his feet are never a moment quiet and in short, his whole person is in *perpetual motion*.' Burney's genuine delight in the originality of individuals evolves as a genius for trenchant character demolition in her novels, in targets such as the bumptious social climber, Mr Smith, the inspired lunatic, Mr Dubster and the filthy miser, Mr Briggs, whose personalities are fleshed from her perception of physical curiosities.

It is Fanny Burney's comic flair which helps to distinguish her novels from those of her contemporaries. A keen lover of theatre, she was obviously influenced by dramatic practice, not only in characterisation but in her conception of the comic possibilities of situation. Despite her image of ladylike propriety, her humour is raucous and often outrageous. Her novels contain scenes of wild farce, unthinkable for later women writers with their controlled decorousness. The dropping of an old woman's wig and the overturning of a carriage provide Burney with occasions for laughter, if they demonstrate the discomfiture of haughty or vulgar individuals. She had a keen sense of the ridiculous, but it became tempered more and more by notions of artistic decorum, as she grew older and became more urgently aware of the effects of public notice. After the success of *Evelina*, Sir Joshua Reynolds had recommended her to write 'anything in the dialogue way', a proposal strongly endorsed by Sheridan's enthusiastic encouragement. Mrs Thrale's Streatham set were quick to recognise the dramatic potential of *Evelina*, and the result of this heady influence, chasing quickly on *Evelina*'s heels, was the glittering and acerbic *The Witlings*, a tight little play, with highly individualised 'humour' characters: Mrs Voluble, Lady Smatter, Mrs Sapient and Mrs Wheedle. On the title page of this onslaught on the pretensions of female literati, Fanny Burney signed herself 'A Sister of the Order' of Witlings, a self irony which disappointingly vanishes in her later work. Perhaps it was the anxious condemnation of her father and Mr Crisp that awakened her to the thorns in the path of public scrutiny, and made her so nervous about the future reception of her writing. Certainly her native talent for dialogue never diminished. It remained for her an instinctive approach in the visualisation of events, and many of her letters are written in dialogue form, set out like the script of a play, as action acquires meaning through the perception of its participants.

Certainly one of the reasons for the great success of *Evelina* was its dramatised technique, a technique which Burney was to discard in her other novels. In selecting the method she used in her journals for her fiction, she was able to amalgamate most closely the aspects of her divided sensibility, the private and the public selves. When, in her subsequent fiction, she had to find an authoritative voice to describe the events taking place, the efforts of depersonalisation progressively obliterated the essential spontaneity of vision and *The Wanderer*, her last novel, which contains some of the most penetrating political insights, is actually the dullest and most tedious of her books. Both Burney's journals and her first novel, however, assert overpoweringly the centrality of the self in defining the nature of experience. It is personality which shapes our response here, rather than events, and both the diaries and *Evelina* embody the triumph of contingency over form.

These two aspects of her writing, the novels and the diaries, illuminate the difference between material moulded to fit a conventional pattern and material which defines and creates its own pattern. And there is always present in the novels themselves a tension between the dominant moral strictures and the imaginative evocation of personal impressions. This can be detected in the narrative organisation which tries to accommodate both formal, often derivative, motifs and individual subjective insights. The sequence of the four novels demonstrates this tension quite strikingly. *Evelina* freely adapts the techniques of the personal diary to the disciplines of fiction and much of its charm is in the very freshness which the epistolary method throws into prominence, as Evelina's perceptions establish the means by which we see the story. The next three novels, however, reverse this procedure. Burney, much more conscious of the possible criticism from her readers, submerges her heroines' voices beneath an impersonal, authorial commentary. Events therefore gain consequence and become increasingly insistent. Cecilia, for example, moves to London from the country at the beginning of the novel because under the terms of her guardian's will she has no alternative not, like Evelina, because she is invited. As circumstances take over, the quality of the characters' experience is reported rather than enacted. The diction too becomes more dignified, as Fanny Burney seems to lose touch with any direct involvement in the activities she recounts. 'It is not very early in life we learn how little is performed, for which no precaution is taken', the narrator of *Camilla* admonishes her audience. 'Care is the offspring of disappointment; and sorrow and repentance commonly hang upon its first lessons.' This is typical of Burney's later fictional style. Passive constructions, abstract nouns, the didactic tone all combine to try to deny the force of the subjective experience which *Evelina* had so keenly tried to convey. The language moves further and further from the intimacy we find both there and in the letters and journals. Only in the dramatic comedies does it recur, where the genre itself dictates the author's absence and characters can speak freely in their own idiom.

Once again we are faced with Fanny Burney's own difficulty in finding an appropriate role for herself. Her natural genius for dramatisation, like her own gift for mimicry which she suppressed in polite company, became squashed beneath her urge to conform to the proprieties and her attempt to synchronise her own responses with the persona she believed it was her duty to adopt led inevitably to literary disaster. It was as if the freedom to think and speak as she liked was a reward she granted herself for good behaviour; certainly her mischievous opinions were saved for unguarded moments with her diary, her close friends and her family. She screened her private personality, her lifeline, from intrusive public eyes as, dominated by her consciousness of expected codes of feminine reticence, she sensed that her own ideas were at odds with the contemporary ethos.

The forms of her writing mirror their subjects. The examination of how to adapt the private self to a required public role is central to all her work. The problem of how to synthesise individualism with the social ethic can be solved for her only through the device of secrecy. It is important both for Burney and her heroines, to keep hidden the true impulses of the soul, which are essentially uncontained and free. When she was an old lady, she went through her journals, erasing sections and destroying whole years of memories, for fear of possible publication. The fact that private and public lives could never satisfactorily merge became increasingly apparent to her as her work developed. Female freedom is the subject of all her novels and it is a subject which is reflected in the forms those novels take, as they move towards a public voice, a reduction of the writer's own personality and a tone of objective neutrality. As she became more conscious of the demands of the all powerful system which determined the conditions of women's lives, she found that secrecy was her only recourse. Both Fanny Burney's life and her writings ultimately affirm this course of action.

3 Evelina

Subterfuge surrounded the entire production of *Evelina*. Night after night, Fanny Burney sat alone in her room after the rest of the family was asleep, scribbling away at the acerbic portraits and reworking the overheard scraps of conversation that she had entered in her diary, busily transforming them into fiction. As she saw the bones of the novel begin to flesh out, she privately gloated over her secret. 'Distant as you may think us from the great world, I sometimes find myself in the midst of it,' she confided enigmatically in a journal letter to her sister, Susan, 'though nobody suspects the brilliancy of the company I keep!' The resplendent companions in whom she so delighted, Lord Orville, Sir Clement Willoughby, Lady Louisa Larpent and their crew, provided for her a never-ending source of amusement and fed her inventiveness during the long periods of apparent solitude, when her family were away and she had time to devote to herself and her writing.

Burney had been experimenting ever since she was an adolescent with the germs of the story of the unhappy Caroline Evelyn and her daughter but it was probably only during 1774 that she set about reworking it in earnest. By 1776, in collusion with her brother Charles and her sisters, she decided to approach a publisher with the first two volumes, never guessing for one moment the eventual consequences of such a step. Publication seemed an exciting escapade and all sorts of stratagems were resorted to in order to avoid detection. First, Fanny set herself to work, laboriously transcribing the manuscript, disguising her handwriting so that her identity as author could never be suspected. Charles, who delivered the parcel of papers, was himself muffled up beyond recognition and Mr Lowndes, the publisher chosen, was instructed to send all correspondence first to a 'Mr King' and then to a 'Mr Grafton' at an anonymous address. Fear of discovery dogged Fanny and when *Evelina* actually appeared in print, in late January 1778, she became nervous that she had allowed even her aunts and sisters into the secret, for 'I foresaw a thousand dangers of a discovery; – I dreaded the indiscreet warmth of all my confidents. . . . In truth I was quite sick with apprehension'. She shrank from the criticisms she anticipated if she were found out, expecting attacks both on the merit of her 'little book' and on herself, for novel writing still carried the stigma of scandal. It was certainly thought improper for a young woman, brought up in relative seclusion, to claim a wide knowledge of human affairs and the romantic theme could be evidence of an unfortunate propensity for indelicate fantasising. But even more than this, it was the invasion of her privacy that Burney dreaded and when, in March 1778, she heard that *Evelina* was now to be found in all the circulating libraries, the news produced in her 'an exceedingly odd sensation, when I consider that it is now in the power of *any* and *every*body to read what I so carefully hoarded even from my best friends, till this last month or two.' The awful truth was dawning gradually upon her.

On the first counts, her fears were quite groundless. Everywhere her book was acclaimed. 'It is by far the most *bewitching* novel I *ever* read', rapturously exclaimed Elizabeth Burney to Susan, with an inkling of suspicion as to the author. 'I think I know a person not one hundred miles from Leicester Square very capable of writing such a novel',[1] she ventured, familiar with her cousin Fanny's wicked style of mimicry. Dr Burney, however, was completely in the dark. Awakened one morning by strange noises coming from the next room, Susan discovered her father and stepmother laughing uncontrollably, reading *Evelina* together. 'The best

novel I know', commented Dr Burney, 'excepting Fielding's
– and in some respects it is better than his'. But the Burney
household was only echoing the praise to be heard
everywhere. The book was well reviewed in the influential
London journals. Mrs Cholmondely, a noted society hostess,
'never met with so much merit before in any literary
performance' and determined to 'keep it on her table the
whole summer that everybody that knows her may see it – for
she says everybody ought to read it!' Even Dr Johnson
observed that 'there were passages in it which might do
honour to Richardson', from him the highest possible paeon.
Fanny was overwhelmed. Eventually her secret had to be
disclosed to her father, who in turn could not wait to spread
the news of his daughter's success. Fanny Burney's life and
her writing were never to be the same again.

Why should what seems to us now to be a comparatively
modest achievement have been greeted with such
extravagant adulation? Was this slight comedy of manners by
an unknown girl really comparable with the work of the
masters, Richardson and Fielding? Why did it become so
quickly the talk of literary London, so that it was obligatory
reading for both fashionable hostesses and learned scholars?
In order to understand the impact made by *Evelina*, we need
to realise something of the context in which it appeared.
When he finally got to know the truth, Dr Burney was
amazed that a young woman could have produced such a
book given her sex and her inevitably limited knowledge of
life and this sort of attitude did in part help to publicise the
book as something of a phenomenon. But even when they
thought the author was male, the general audience, assessing
it on merit, received the work with wild enthusiasm.

Towards the end of the 1770s, the number of published
novels had declined sharply and a market that until recently
had been swamped with fiction was now desperate for new
productions. Only sixteen new novels appeared in 1776,
compared with sixty, five years earlier. The reading public

were avid for novels but the popular highlights of 1777, the year before *Evelina*, were the sentimental fictions, *Julia de Roubigne* by Henry Mackenzie and Courtney Melmoth's *Travels for the Heart*, wildly successful it is true, but sticking closely to a well-tried and familiar formula. The usual sprinkling of sensational romances and moral tales completed the booksellers' consignment for the year. As Mrs Thrale declared, in such a climate of almost universal mediocrity, *Evelina* clearly excelled all other new novels 'both in probability of story, elegance of sentiment and general power over the mind, whether exerted in humour or in pathos'. The book satisfied the criteria of all best sellers: it had something for everyone. It combined the psychological realism of Richardson with the satiric comedy of Fielding and could therefore be read with equal pleasure by young ladies and their fathers. It was both funny and sad, often simultaneously, so that readers were torn between laughter and tears at Evelina's confusion and inexperience. It perfectly blended moral sentiment, in the characters of Villars and Orville, with sharp dramatic cartoons which mirrored and formed a comment on a whole range of social mores so that Burney was able to appear to endorse and to expose social attitudes at one and the same time, a masterly achievement. Fanny Burney had caught precisely the requirements of her age, assimilating effortlessly the features of the popular literary forms she had encountered so that they acquired a new dimension. In a time of waning confidence in fiction, *Evelina* restored faith in the capacity of the novel as a serious literary genre. The only adverse criticism was that the book was too short and one young lady was heard to complain bitterly that she had read the whole thing in a mere two days!

Briefly, *Evelina*'s story is that of a young country girl's initiation into polite London society. Her mother, secretly married to the wealthy Sir John Belmont, has died in childbirth and Evelina Anville, abandoned by her father and his family who disapproved of the marriage, has been

brought up in rural seclusion by her guardian, the Rev. Mr
Villars. Invited to London by friends, she is at once
introduced to fashionable pursuits and customs as well as to
the world of men, represented most notably by the
honourable hero, Lord Orville, and the rakish villain, Sir
Clement Willoughby. Evelina's understanding of the
mechanisms of social advancement is complicated by the
arrival on the scene of her maternal grandmother, the
outrageously vulgar Mme Duval and her relatives, the even
cruder Branghton family, who live ignominiously up two
flights of stairs in Holborn and who seem determined to
embarrass Evelina by flaunting their kinship and their
ill-breeding on occasions when she is especially keen to
impress her new aristocratic friends. After a series of
mishaps, Evelina gets both the husband she wants, Lord
Orville, and the family who have rejected her from birth. She
is reunited with her father and on the way has managed to
discover a brother in similar circumstances to herself. At the
end of the novel, she is able to erase the mortifying memory
of her association with the disreputable Branghtons and can
feel secure with her new name and her new position as
Evelina Belmont, soon to be Orville.

Even from such a summary, it is possible to recognise the
elements which so charmed the reading public that, before
the end of 1779, the novel had run into four editions and was
still in constant demand in libraries and booksellers, in
London and in all the best watering places. The romantic
myth of rags to riches was completely absorbed within a
realistic presentation and an analysis of social forms which
never seriously disturbed the status quo. Fanny Burney
ridicules snobbery – she has no time for pretentiousness or
assumed airs – but in so doing, she herself exhibits attitudes
which implicitly support the rigidity of the class system.
Evelina is only seeking her rights in wanting a top-drawer
husband – it is mere accident that her innate sense of
refinement is not backed up by the authority of an

established family. In exposing the vulgarity of the comic Mr Smith and the Branghtons, Burney clears the way for a parallel explanation of the constituents of gentility in Evelina but always the social divisions are perceived as fixed, the hierarchy is accepted and there is no apparent questioning of the fundamental structure. Rather, Evelina's progress is presented as a growing understanding of the real power of the social apparatus. 'I knew not till now', she writes ruefully to her guardian, 'how requisite are birth and fortune to the attainment of respect and civility'. Her graceful behaviour and solidly imbued moral standards are insufficient on their own terms to win her full acceptance.

In her diary for 1778, Fanny Burney explained her approach in a typically defensive manner. 'I have not pretended to shew the world what it actually *is*', she pleaded, 'but what it *appears* to a girl of seventeen: – and so far as that, surely any girl who is *past* seventeen may safely do?' In this aim, she was entirely successful. Evelina's letters differ from those in many earlier epistolary fictions in their total credibility. Never for a moment do they appear to be an awkward, adopted narrative device, which constricts the author and offers a one-sided, limited view of events. Evelina's daily effusions are impulsive and exhilarating. They capture completely the excitements and impressionability of the young girl's awakening to heady new experiences and illuminate their meaning by dramatising how, for individuals, trivia gains significance. 'Let us not take it for granted', Virginia Woolf was later to write in her spirited defence of modern fiction, 'that life exists more fully in what is commonly thought big than in what is commonly thought small'.[2] Fanny Burney's method takes this truth for granted and because Evelina, in her naivety, is absolutely honest about what she records, we are able to respond to her critically, while retaining a degree of imaginative identification with her personal life. The careful selectivity of her correspondence points us also towards a range of further levels of meaning.

In presenting urban life through the medium of her heroine's perception, Burney explores the discrepancies that exist between moral theory and social practice. Evelina's letters home, fresh and ingenuous, are a measure of her empiricism against Mr Villars' idealism. She is mobile; he is static. Her experiences are at first hand: his are at a remove. The confrontation between town and country values is used by Burney to demonstrate the problematics of a conceptual morality, given the conditions of contemporary urban living. Mr Villars, who dwells in retirement, finds it easy to base his values upon absolutes. His judgements, distanced from Evelina's daily life, form a backdrop for the dramatic projection of her actual experiences and sometimes prove fallible. His view of Lord Orville, for instance, is cautious, indirect and mistaken, as compared with Evelina's assessment which is based unerringly on her direct personal response. In trying to come to terms with the complexities of social morality, the novel constantly affirms the validity of individual experience.

But the county/town opposition is not only used for purposes of ethical analysis. London is seen as necessary. It is the centre of power and energy and Evelina's first impression of the city is of a vital and stimulating nucleus, an impression which becomes tempered as the novel develops but which is never totally disabused. Nature versus Art is Burney's theme and she reworks the topical Rousseauesque confrontation between natural innocence and corrupt civilisation to show the impact on the young free mind of the formal disciplines of organised society. Coming from her sober and straightforward upbringing, Evelina is initially enchanted by London which unfolds before her eyes as a series of ingeniously devised entertainments: the theatre, the opera, the dance, the ridotto, the puppets, the museum with its mechanical birds. All are glosses on the raw material of life and London itself materialises as a theatre, where the characters are players on show, wearing masks that create their public identities. It constantly imitates itself, selecting and moulding the basic ingredients to new designs. London in fact transforms life and makes it into a game with elaborate rules which must be obeyed or the player is disqualified. It both refines and perverts nature and its magnetism, though attractive, must be treated with discrimination.

This understanding of the power of form dominates the novel. At the basis of Evelina's quandary is the problem of how to amalgamate her natural, meaningful values to the often artificial demands of civilised life. From the beginning of the story, much is made of her lack of polish. 'She is quite a little rustic and knows nothing of the world', Mr Villars warns his friends. 'She is innocent as an angel and artless as purity itself.' *Natural, simple, ingenuous, artless*: these are words which recur time and again in the early stages of the novel to establish the momentum for the action. But the long journal letters that Evelina sends to Mr Villars have a further purpose. Indubitably they present the collision between nature and art, innocence and experience, youth and maturity but they also identify this as a discrepancy between the distinctively female viewpoint of Evelina and the patriarchal system she encounters. Thus the narrative method itself becomes the very subject of the book; the way in which a young woman perceives.

As Dr Burney most acutely recognised, Evelina is 'not indeed like most modern young ladies, to be known in half an hour'. *Artless*, naive and inexperienced for much of the time, Evelina is yet the most ambivalent of eighteenth-century heroines. In accordance with the theatrical imagery which packs the novel, she too must learn to play a role and from the start she proves herself an adept at this. Outwardly she conforms to the masculine ideal of womanhood: she is the embodiment of the pallid courtesy book figure created by male fantasy – childlike, dutiful, modest and limp. But by establishing the narrative in Evelina's consciousness, Fanny Burney is able to show her simultaneously as perceptive, independent, critical and mentally alert. In different ways she is both passive and active. Clearly she has a strong and well-defined personality but her intelligence and wit are allowed to function only within prescribed limits. As far as her public behaviour is concerned, she persists in an attitude of helplessness, reliant on male advice. It is only in her letters that her perspicacity and sound judgement emerge. The whole action of the novel therefore contains something of a paradox. Evelina is easily the most astute and reliable character around but she remains subservient to the cardboard figures who masquerade as men, asking them to 'think for me, my dearest Sir, and suffer not my doubting mind that knows not which way to direct its hopes to be guided by your wisdom and unerring counsel.' Evelina surely needs no-one to think for her; her quizzical intelligence selects and discriminates on every page of the novel. Rather, albeit unconsciously, she is playing a double game.

Burney's novels all assert the power of the conventions and the presentation of her heroines demonstrates her concern with the adaptation of the individual to the group, rather than the search for any escape from it. Burney was always sensitive to the dangers inherent in flouting convention. When in 1799 her brother, James, left his wife and children to live in a semi-incestuous idyll with his half-sister, Sarah, Fanny Burney's reaction was not that of a prude, shocked by sexual aberration. Her condemnation was harsh, but it was reserved for 'the rash selfishness with which they have broken through all duties to others for their own singular caprice and inclination.' This concern with social duty deeply worried her and it forms a central thematic strand in *Evelina*, which considers the difficulties which beset conformism and questions how a woman can retain her sense

of individual identity while gaining social approval. From
Evelina's situation as outcast, with nothing but her personal
accomplishments to recommend her, she has to gain her
place as an accepted member of the community to which she
aspires. This acceptance, so vital to her eventual comfort and
economic security, can, she discovers, be achieved only by
her adherence to the approved stereotype.

Her search for approval coincidentally reveals the tensions
that exist between her need for protection and her private
opinions of the society on whose mercies she is thrown.
Evelina approaches her first ball with feelings of trepidation
but mixed with the wonder at the splendour of the occasion is
shock and revulsion.

'The gentlemen, as they passed and repassed, looked as if
they thought we were quite at their disposal, and only
waiting for the honour of their commands; and they
sauntered about, in a careless, indolent manner, as if with a
view to keeping us in suspense . . . and I thought it so
provoking, that I determined, in my own mind, that, far
from humouring such airs, I would not dance at all, than
with anyone who should seem to think me ready to accept
the first partner who would condescend to take me.'

Evelina instinctively objects to the assumption that women
are passive ladies-in-waiting and men the active masters. But
this is the world that makes the rules and her determination
to retain her capacity for choice leads to disaster. When she
rejects a ridiculous and impertinent fop who asks her to
dance and instead accepts the courteous Orville, her
ignorance of behavioural codes is a blunder which lays her
open to the charge of illbreeding and might well prejudice
her chances of ultimate success. At the end of the evening,
'tired, ashamed and mortified' she is overcome with
embarrassment. Evelina has had to learn the price of being a
participant instead of a mere spectator in the sectarian game

of life. In future she must limit her criticism to her personal correspondence and this she sustains unflaggingly.

In utilising the epistolary form, Fanny Burney develops the Richardsonian emphasis on individual experience to highlight the dichotomy that exists between private and public levels of activity. In *Evelina*, women's social experience is seen explicitly as a form of role-playing, duplicitous because while eager for approbation, Evelina's letters provide a continuous critique of the male dominated society, bringing to light and ridiculing its affectation and injustice. 'A terrible reverse of the order of nature!' she observes about her new lifestyle. 'We sleep with the sun and wake with the moon' and her attack is remorselessly maintained on the deviant and artificial. Male poseurs abound; the shop assistants, who 'seemed to understand every part of a woman's dress better than we do ourselves'; the gourmets 'dainty and voracious', who sicken her by their excesses; the men of fashion whose habit of wagering undermines the value of money, 'since those who possess it squander it away in a manner so infinitely absurd!' Evelina's original delight in the show that London provides gradually sours as her experience widens. Her second visit to the theatre is in sharp contrast to her first magical vision of Garrick, for the play, *Love For Love*, 'is so extremely indelicate' that it is an affront to modesty and the female hold on innocence. That this hold is a tenuous one is affirmed by each successive event.

The keenly anticipated parties that Evelina attends in actuality expose her to ostentatious gallantry from men who patronise her with empty, extravagant compliments and her only available response is to turn 'away from this nonsense with real disgust'. Without the means of retaliation she recoils but although her judgement never falters her conduct does adjust itself to expected patterns of propriety. On that second theatre outing, she remains silent, despite being close to tears, when a dandified nobleman insults her with

unwarrantable freedom, mocking her as a country bumpkin.
Now, humiliated and acknowledging that he is 'malicious
and impertinent', she knows that she cannot fight back.
Gone are the irrepressible giggles of her early scenes. 'I am
sure I hope I shall never see him again', she writes bitterly to
Mr Villars after this ordeal. 'I should have despised him
heartily as a fop, had he never spoken to me at all; but now,
that he thinks proper to resent his supposed ill-usage, I am
really quite afraid of him.' Fear has come to predominate
over discrimination. Men are recognised as powerful and
influential arbitrators and she is advised by a cynical friend to
pay court to the man who has most openly vilified her, for
'though he is malicious, he is fashionable, and may do you
some harm in the great world.' Evelina's silence becomes
eloquent testimony to her acquiescence to endurance.

Her disaffection is instead given voice by another woman
character, one whose own social position is assured and who
can thus afford the luxury of speaking her mind. Mrs Selwyn
is the first in the line of Burney's clever women, a type which
clearly fascinated her and which receives somewhat
equivocal attention in all her novels. Mrs Delvile in *Cecilia*,
Mrs Arlbery in *Camilla* and Elinor Joddrel in *The Wanderer*
are all extended versions of the independent and self-assured
Mrs Selwyn who escorts Evelina to Bristol Hotwells.
Forceful, intelligent and oblivious to the general disapproval
of the company, she completely rejects the requisite standard
model of feminine behaviour. She is openly derisive about
the idea of weakness and sensibility in women, addresses
men on equal terms, and engages victoriously in verbal
repartee with those who are foolish enough to take her on.
Her wit and fluency are able champions of Evelina's
inarticulacy. 'Pray my Lord', appeals Evelina ineffectually to
an over-assiduous admirer, 'let go my hand! pray, Mrs.
Selwyn, speak for me.' 'My Lord', said Mrs Selwyn, 'in
detaining Miss Anville any longer, you only lose time, for we
are already as well convinced of your valour and your

strength as if you were to hold her an age.' In the same way
that later women writers were to exploit to the full the
resources of irony, Mrs Selwyn's sarcasm is her weapon
against the physical superiority of men but Evelina's attitude
towards her dynamism remains uncertain.

> She is extremely clever; her understanding, indeed may be
> called *masculine*; but unfortunately, her manners deserve
> the same epithet; for in studying to acquire the knowledge
> of the other sex, she has lost all the softness of her own.

Evelina's comment reflects Burney's diffidence in endorsing
the unwomanly woman. Despite her evident admiration for
Mrs Selwyn's intellectual toughness, she feels she has to
portray her as deficient in sensitivity. It is obviously a
problem for Burney, writing in 1778, to create an aggressive
woman who is also sympathetic, given the contemporary
prejudices about female militancy. 'Is that queer woman
your mother?' enquires one young man of Evelina and she is
ready to die with the shame of the association. Significantly,
however, it is Mrs Selwyn who engineers Evelina's
reconciliation with her father and who insists on her rightful
inheritance. Mr Villars, 'disgusted' at Mrs Selwyn's
'unmerciful propensity to satire', has been unable for the past
seventeen years to bring off the success that she achieves in a
matter of weeks. So we are presented with two models of
female behaviour and Mrs Selwyn must be seen as a
necessary complement to Evelina. The older woman's
eloquence needs to be balanced against the silence of the
younger, for the novel demonstrates that active interference
produces results just as effectively as the heroine's modest
submissiveness secures the attentions of the desirable Lord
Orville. From her position of profound insecurity, Evelina
needs to cultivate the conventional image of compliance but,
through the use of Mrs Selwyn as prime agent in Evelina's

final achievement, Burney suggests her dismay at having to sanction such a philosophy.

As Sandra Gilbert and Susan Gubar have argued in their study of the nineteenth century, several later women writers have shown that 'female survival depends on gaining male approval and protection'.[3] Fanny Burney early recognised this uncomfortable truth. For the other side of the coin is that Evelina's gaucherie, the very quality which causes her so much concern, forms the source of her attraction for Lord Orville. 'I am charmed', said he, 'at the novelty of meeting with one so unhackneyed in the world, as not yet to be influenced by custom to forget the use of reason.' Her perception of a society which has lost contact with both rationalism and feeling is confirmed by his support. Her spontaneity is her prime asset but ironically she has to restrain and modify it before she can win the man she needs.

At the beginning of the novel, Evelina's impulses combine sensitivity with an evaluative penetration. Her emotions are alive; compassion and sympathy are second nature to her; but she is also intolerant of stupidity, finds the distortions of sense farcical and has no respect for mindless conventions. To her, human foibles are funny; she views people as performers in the comedy of life and even Lord Orville is initially not exempt from her merriment. When, at her first ball, she sees 'such extreme surprise in his face – the cause of which appeared so absurd, that I could not for my life preserve my gravity,' Orville is clearly put out by such licence and Evelina is soon made to realise her error. A later episode, the dance at the Hampstead Assembly with the Branghtons, shows Evelina herself adopting his stentorian position and she condemns outright the vulgar Mr Smith who, faced with the outrageous spectacle of the rigged out Mme Duval, 'was so ill-bred as to laugh at her very openly . . . but I would neither look nor listen to him; nor would I suffer him to proceed with a speech which he began.' Evelina has moved from a positive to a negative approach to experience. Her language has become the language of denial and repression. In mastering the rules of etiquette, she has come to realise that certain of her natural responses are unacceptable. She never loses her capacity for discernment but she learns to control its reprehensible effects and to acquire silence, gravity and composure, the components of good breeding that Lord Orville particularly admires.

In his alleged dislike of artifice, Orville is the urban representative of the values that Mr Villars encodes in his country retreat. His remark on architecture encapsulates the version of ideal elegance that the novel proposes, 'when . . . the eye may be regaled at the same time and in one view, with all the excellence of art and all the perfection of nature, I cannot think that either suffer by being seen together.' Evelina can only attain this immaculate combination of art and nature by suppressing those elements in her personality which are socially discreditable. By the end of the book, she has become like one of the birds in Cox's museum, barely distinguishable from the real thing but operated by an imposed mechanism to best please the spectators.

All Evelina can do to captivate Orville is to maximise her assets. She plays on the image of helplessness, flattering him as a superior being and making much of her own sense of inferiority, socially, morally and intellectually. For above all, Evelina wants a champion and with an inadequate father of her own she finds in Orville a perfect substitute for Villars. Even his name suggests his appropriateness as replacement. For Burney, romance takes second place to the economic and moral stability that men can provide. In her early diary, she confessed that 'My father and Mr Crisp spoil me for every other male creature' and these two men are transformed into the heroes of her first novel. Youthful virility becomes almost a deficiency in Burney's portrayal of the masculine ideal, for Evelina visualises Orville as he will be 'when time has wintered o'er his locks' and she compares him directly and rather unfavourably with her elderly guardian at Berry Hill.

'I sometimes imagine' she longingly fantasises, 'that when his youth is flown, his vivacity abated, and his life is devoted to retirement, he will perhaps resemble him whom I most love and honour'. While her relations with her actual lover are formal and restrained, confined to reading, polite conversation and the rituals of the dance, her behaviour both with her father, Sir John Belmont, and her guardian verges on sexual hysteria. 'With a pleasure that bordered upon agony, I embraced his knees', she writes, describing her meeting with Villars after a few weeks' absence. 'I kissed his hands, I wept over them, while he, holding me in his arms. . . .' These are not the raptures of impassioned lovers but the asexual greeting of guardian and ward. Evelina's emotions are given free rein in the relationship that protects and Orville qualifies as a lover only when he can be safely identified with a father figure.

Whatever the personal, psychological sources of such a position, Burney perceives socially that sex is dangerous. A woman, entering the 'world' for the first time is seen as easy prey and the values of individualism that Burney would like to endorse are inadequate weapons to fight the threats that surround it. Men may be mostly fools but they are powerful fools. Sir Clement Willoughby uses the veneer of civility to conceal his true intention to seduce Evelina; Mr Lovel can freely insult her without rebuke; even Mr Smith is part of the conspiracy to degrade and manipulate female vulnerability. For all these men act on the assumption that women are theirs for the taking and female sexuality is used to focus the uncertainties that surround female identity. Sir Clement believes that Evelina has deliberately sought out the tantalising dark alleys at Vauxhall. At Marybone Gardens, the secluded walks are the known haunts of prostitutes and Evelina becomes indistinguishable from their number when she finds herself unwittingly in their company. Respectability becomes difficult to maintain in the face of such blurred definitions. The code of conduct Fanny Burney proposes in this novel is clear-sighted and prudential. In understanding just how easy it is to lose one's way at Marybone Gardens, or indeed anywhere, she deals directly with women's need for social protection and her message is communicated with a wry intensity.

In many ways, Fanny Burney is an unsophisticated artist, unaware that she is projecting her own mechanisms for survival through her fictional characters. Like her creation, Mrs Selwyn, Fanny Burney finds that comedy is often her best means of defence against the system and *Evelina* is frequently a most provocative novel in its unusual amalgamation of contradictory elements. Like the heroine, it appears to conform meekly to certain contemporary conventions, with a romantic plot, a banished heiress and an egregious patrician hero. At odds with this overt romantic direction, however, is a strong vein of wild and earthy comedy. Anarchic and often violent in its nature, it suggests the threat of disruption beneath the controlled surface. The introduction of the Holborn episodes, for instance, allows Burney the opportunity for unrestrained and scathing mockery of ignorance, insensitivity and folly. Her characters, 'all smart and gaudy, so pert and ill-bred', reveal their limitations with every word and action. But the humour does not rest with the sharp observance of tone or gesture. The satire is direct and vicious and the style veers towards slapstick, farce and bawdry. There is a relish of physical humiliation with its accompanying unpleasant images: Mme Duval trussed in a ditch; M. du Bois soused in a horse pond. When the cloak of polite gentility is removed, Burney's world becomes one of practical jokers, raucous laughter, coarse familiarity and blunt language. Her characters flaunt their grossness: they are rude, dirty, uncontrolled and are consequently exhibited as clowns. Embarrassment is made a constant source of uneasy laughter and Burney exploits to the full the ambivalent potential of the contrast between Evelina's delicacy and the vulgarity around her. How are we supposed to react, for example, to Evelina's being forced to witness intimacies between Miss Polly Branghton and her lover?

> . . . as soon as the common enquiries were over, Mr Brown grew so fond, and so foolish, that I was extremely disgusted. Polly, all the time, only rebuked him with, 'La, now, Mr Brown, do be quiet, can't you? – you should not behave so before company. – Why now what will Miss think of me?'

Burney's ability to include such scenes helps to make her the double-edged writer she is, as the overall decorum of the novel is undermined by the uncomfortable quality of the satire. *Evelina* is a crucial novel in the history of women's literature. It mirrors Burney's dilemma as a woman writer by taking and using the idea of subterfuge as a defence. Burney's own acerbity is made acceptable by being contained within the comic spirit and this in turn is diluted within the mask of conventionalism that the novel formally adopts. Both the narrative technique and the central character apparently conform to the male canon of femininity. The heroine's 'nature' is set against the world's 'art' and seems to triumph. But the real appeal of the novel resides not in the heroine's sensibility, which in any case is exaggerated to satisfy expectation, but in her and her creator's firmness, decision, rational thought, insight and comic flair, the very reverse of the 'feminine' ideal.

4 Cecilia

Towards the end of *Cecilia*, in the fifth volume, Mr Belfield laments the drudgery of the hack writer. All the joys he used to find in literature, and the imaginative delights of creativity, have been eroded for him by the insistent pressures of professionalism. It is now anguish, he grumbles to Cecilia,

> 'to write by rule, to compose by necessity, to make the understanding, nature's first gift, subservient to interest . . . when weary, listless, spiritless, to rack the head for invention, the memory for images, and the fancy for ornament and allusion, and when the mind is wholly occupied by its own affections and affairs, to call forth all its faculties for foreign subjects, uninteresting discussions, or fictitious incidents!'

The bitterness of the complaint is clearly heartfelt. By the time Fanny Burney came to write this, she had experienced the dubious rewards of fame and public notice and the conditions in which *Cecilia* was produced were very different from the leisurely methods which had contributed to the fun of *Evelina*.

From start to finish, the composition of *Cecilia* was a struggle. Fanny Burney's progress, no longer confined to the relaxed privacy of her own room, was carefully monitored by the hawklike scrutiny of her father and Mr Crisp, ever watchful of the reputation of their protégée. Not only this but Fanny's new status as a celebrity encroached into her precious time. Even her journal suffered. 'Don't be angry that I have been absent so long without writing', she apologised to her father from Bath, where she had been taken by the ardent Mrs Thrale who had by now more or less adopted Fanny, 'for I have been so entirely without a moment to myself, except for dressing, that I really have not had it in my power.' Invitations and plaudits were heaped upon her and, at the best of times diffident in company, she found herself nonplussed at having become so suddenly the centre of attention among strangers. Added to this were family traumas: the savage anti-Catholic Gordon riots around the Burney home in London; her brother Charles' mounting debts; Susan's marriage and the implication of the sisters' separation; her stepmother's near fatal illness. Devoted to her family, Fanny took these problems deeply to heart and worried desperately that she could not be on hand to help. For several months, Mr Crisp secluded her at his home at Chessington to keep her nose firmly to the grindstone but the result was only to increase her sense of strain. 'One way or other my hand scarce rests an hour in the whole day', she wrote pathetically to Susan. 'I begin to grow horribly tired & yet am by no means near anything bordering upon an end. And the eternal fagging of my mind and brains does really much mischief to my health.' And indeed, worn out with fatigue and anxiety, Fanny became seriously ill during much of 1781, working herself up as well into a frenzy of worry over her father's reaction to her shortcomings, but despite all of this the writing of *Cecilia*, begun towards the end of 1780 and finished early in 1782, was completed remarkably in little more than a year.

Inevitably, the constraints that had surrounded her affected the quality of the eventual product and *Cecilia* lacks the spontaneous ebullience that had so enlivened *Evelina*. Much longer than the first novel, it suffered too from a lack of adequate revision. Mr Crisp had in the past admonished Fanny about her tendency to be 'devilish long-winded' but to correct her verbosities and to strive for economy she needed time and this was denied her. Her audience and her publishers alike were eager to see her new work and booksellers wanted the usual five volumes to swell their profits. *Evelina*, written without any real thought of its possible market was unusual in having only three and in judging Burney's later novels, we must bear in mind the style and demands of the age, which was voracious for lengthy reading matter, as well as her own inbred deference to others' opinions about artistic proprieties.

In many ways though, *Cecilia* is actually a great improvement on *Evelina*. Fanny Burney's wider experience of life had produced a correspondingly greater maturity of vision and the book is both more direct and more energetic in its social criticism than *Evelina*. In abandoning the epistolary form and adopting instead a detached narrative voice, Burney allowed herself the liberty of artistic distance. She was able to create a definitive moral environment for her characters and although she misses the opportunities to exploit the ironic potential of the authorial tone, she still permits the comic spirit to dominate and to brighten the savagery of much of her social satire. This is largely because of her reliance on dramatic techniques, which take over and vivify large sections of dialogue and action in the novel. Like its heroine, the book is less naive than *Evelina* and more assured and its success was immediate and sensational. An outstanding best seller, it brought its creator uncomfortable fame and a degree of lionisation she found difficult to accept. She suffered agonies of embarrassment when her novel was referred to on stage while she was in a theatre audience. 'Instantly I shrank back', she confessed to her journal, 'so astonished and ashamed of my public situation that I was almost ready to take to my heels and run, for it seemed as if I were there purposely in that conspicuous place – 'To list attentive to my own applause!' 'Next to the balloon, Miss Burney was the object of public curiosity',[1] confirmed Mrs Barbauld, that sharp-eyed observer of literary fashion, after the publication of *Cecilia* and, in an unashamed fan letter, the eminent Edmund Burke shrewdly endorsed the praises that were showered on her both as an artist and as a woman. 'In an age distinguished by producing extraordinary women, I hardly dare tell you where my opinion would place you amongst them', he wrote to her in mock humility in July 1782, going on to give full credit to her personal shyness, for 'I respect your modesty, that will not endure the commendations which your merit forces from everybody.'[2]

The novel opens with the twenty-year-old heiress, Cecilia Beverley, left alone in the world after the death of her uncle with whom she has lived quietly in the country. He has appointed three guardians to look after her welfare until she should reach her twenty-first birthday, when the management of her estate will be her own. The only condition attached to this is that when she marries, her husband, contrary to custom, must take her name or her inheritance will be forfeit. The story follows Cecilia's adventures in London during the next few months, as she meets in turn each of the three guardians and tests out their different value systems. Being a noted heiress, she is also introduced to (and has foisted upon her) a range of prospective suitors for her hand but the clause in the will becomes a serious impediment to her announcing her marriage with the one she chooses, Mortimer Delvile, son of her proud and aristocratic guardian, whose family equate their name with their tradition of honour. Against her better judgement, Cecilia allows herself to be persuaded into a secret marriage but misunderstandings accumulate and, believing herself to be abandoned by Mortimer, Cecilia gradually loses control of the situation, her money and her sanity. The ultimate happy ending of the book is only achieved after Burney averts a melodramatic pile up of near catastrophes.

The effects of the novel were far reaching and numerous works which appeared after *Cecilia* showed evidence of their debt to the situations and personalities which Burney created. Certainly the most famous is *Pride and Prejudice*, written in 1796, in which can be detected several motifs which had appeared in the earlier novel. The words 'pride and prejudice' themselves appear prominently in the closing pages of *Cecilia*; Mortimer Delvile's haughty proposal of marriage is reminiscent of Darcy's more notorious one; Mrs Delvile's intervention to save her son from what she believes to be an ignominious match can be read as a parallel to Lady Catherine de Bourgh's glittering scene with Elizabeth at Longbourn. But these are only details and one can find like parallels in a range of other novels of the time. Charlotte Smith's *Emmeline*, for instance, focuses on the theme of family pride as a barrier to marriage in a very similar way to Burney's use of the Delvile–Cecilia relationship but this was a favourite stand-by anyway of eighteenth-century novelists. Far more significant in considering the influential effect of *Cecilia* is to note the way in which later writers, and Jane Austen in particular, developed and substantiated the realist vision that Fanny Burney introduced.

Cecilia forms a sustained enquiry into the nature and possibilities of women's independence and, throughout the novel, the heroine's story is set against the background of a society dominated by economic issues. In this context, we should perhaps remember the opening sentence of *Pride and Prejudice* and the emphasis in that work on the importance of money as a determinant in social relations. Both Fanny Burney and Jane Austen present their moral evaluation in these texts via details of financial transactions and human problems become illuminated by the use of the imagery of economics. *Cecilia* is centrally about money and inheritance and in it Burney examines the level of control the heroine can exert over her own future, given certain irreversible conditions. *Pride and Prejudice*, with its portionless heroine, concerns itself with the idea of female dispossession and the threat of Mr Collins and the Longbourn entail demonstrates the legal constraints on women's rights to full independence.

Fanny Burney's vision in *Cecilia* is shaped by her recognition of legal injustice and economic reality. Although differently presented, the same recognition informs Jane Austen's work and is taken up and explored by her with the full force of ironic complexity. In many ways Fanny Burney initiated the tradition of women's writing that fourteen years afterwards Jane Austen was able to draw on so confidently and, if we find Burney's own approach now somewhat tentative, we should not allow this to blind us to the seminal aspects of her innovatory viewpoint.

For *Cecilia* does form a challenge to patriarchal values and throughout the book the male world is seen as unreliable and shifting. One of Cecilia's first encounters with metropolitan life is a public sale of a bankrupt's house contents. At once the climate of the novel is established as pointing the fragility of economic survival. There is frequent reference to precise cash sums: Cecilia pays £250 per year for her board and lodging; £10 will clothe and educate the needy Hill children; it costs Mrs Hill £60 to buy a partnership in a small business; the building contractor, who has to pay his workmen on a daily rate, is owed £400 for erecting a theatre at the Harrel's house. The comparative and cumulative sense of the cost of living pervades a range of social strata at a very practical level.

But Burney attacks the most extreme aspects of this reliance on money which becomes a full frontal onslaught on the commercial society. For *Cecilia* is written as a moral fable, set firmly in a cold, realistic world. The princess-like heroine, endowed with beauty, wealth and moral perfection – a model for Jane Austen to turn neatly on its head with 'handsome, clever and rich' Emma Woodhouse – is provided with three male guardians, each deficient in his own way. The spendthrift, Harrel, Cecilia's first guardian, frantic to keep up with the fashionable rich, loses all sense of moral proportion in his extravagance. Lying and cheating, under the guise of courtesy, and playing on her compassion, he induces the susceptible Cecilia to part with vast sums of money from her estate and to pledge herself to grasping moneylenders. The enormity of his debts ultimately overwhelms him and in a series of psychologically convincing scenes, his desperation is shown mounting until he finally commits suicide. In comic contrast, the second guardian, Mr Briggs, is so mean that he lives without light or heat, feeds on scraps and treats his servants like animals. His excessive stinginess disgusts Cecilia as much as Mr Harrel's mindless squandering. She recoils in horror from the bedroom he offers for her use, 'the most forlorn she had ever beheld, containing no other furniture than a ragged stuff bed, two worn-out rush bottomed chairs, an old wooden box, and an old bit of broken glass which was fastened to the wall by two bent nails.' Yet his wealth is enormous, amassed through clever business acumen, and he seeks out a hugely rich, though old and ugly, husband for her. Both Harrel and Briggs demonstrate the moral point that materialism is reductive and dehumanising, while the third guardian, Delvile, to whom Cecilia turns for protection is obsessed with family pride which distorts his perception of natural values.

This sort of satire, though well done, is in itself fairly conventional stuff. Where Fanny Burney becomes quite original is in her explicit association of women with economic issues. The episode of the Hill family, for instance, highlights the specifically female plight of a woman's attempt to survive without a male breadwinner. Mrs Hill's husband, a carpenter, is ill, having fallen from a ladder at work; her only son has died of consumption. When Cecilia first visits them, she discovers, 'five children, all girls, the three eldest of whom were hard at work with their mother in matting chair bottoms, and the fourth, though a mere child, was nursing the youngest.' Burney depicts the struggle to retain domestic order, while also trying to support themselves when their main source of income is removed. The pattern of male death and the resulting female inheritance is a recurrent one in the novel, focusing most notably on Cecilia herself but

seen also in Mrs Harrel, who, ruined by her husband's
extravagance, is left behind after his death to cope with the
consequences of his actions. Time after time, Burney's
women are confronted with practical problems outside the
range of experience they have been trained to deal with.

The argument is pursued with a slightly different
emphasis in the portrayal of female sacrifice in the middle-
class Belfield household. With six daughters and one son,
this family have lavished education and attention on the boy
at the expense of the girls. The result of this partiality is that,
after his father's death, the son, having been given ideas and
tastes beyond his means, despises trade as ignoble and the
family fortunes dwindle accordingly. The only unmarried
sister, Henrietta, bred in the school of female self-denial,
devotes herself to caring for her mother and her misguided
and selfish brother. Interestingly, Burney does not make her
into the heroine of the novel, although she is in many ways
the archetype of the young woman of sensibility, but treats
her as an object of pity, the uncomplaining victim of an
unbalanced and prejudicial society.

Prejudice is what Cecilia must face as she attempts to retain
control of her independence. 'Poor female victim!', shrieks
Albany, addressing Cecilia at her first public appearance like
some sort of choric voice from the wings. 'Seest not that thou
art marked for sacrifice! Yet knowest not that thou art
destined for prey!' Cecilia's innocence is of a very different
quality from Evelina's or from Henrietta Belfield's. It is not a
moral nor a behavioural guide she needs but a financial one.
Her error is to misunderstand the attitude towards women in
this commercially orientated society, for her fortune cannot
protect her from the insulting patronage of male inferiors.
'As to a lady', taunts the vulgar Mr Hobson, 'let her be worth
never so much, she's a mere nobody as one may say 'til she
gets herself a husband, being she knows nothing of business,
and is made to pay for everything through the nose.'

And it is true. Most of the men that Cecilia meets are either trying to defraud her, like Harrel, or are blatant fortune-hunters, like Sir Robert Floyer, who see her as fair game or a prize to be won at cards. Burney reserves some of her most merciless satire for the male propensity to so categorise women. Mr Monckton, the dissembling villain of the novel, moans to his friends about his elderly rich wife's longevity. 'An old woman' they agree, 'is a person who has no sense of decency; if once she takes to living, the devil himself can't get rid of her.' Monckton's attitude is taken to be the norm, and indeed historical accounts bear Burney out. For instance, as Roy Porter has quoted,

> Married, the Rev. Mr. Roger Waind, of York, about twenty-six years of age, to a Lincolnshire lady, upwards of eighty, with whom he is to have £8,000 in money, £300 per annum and a coach-and-four during life only.[3]

was a typical inclusion in a public list of marriage announcements in a contemporary newspaper, when the lady's name wasn't thought to be even worth the bother of printing. Continually in *Cecilia* men are seen as dehumanising women, reducing them to commodities, objects of pleasure or means of income, and it is in such a context that Cecilia must struggle to assert her sense of personal value. Male and female worlds are constantly opposed, and it is only the most exceptional men who are shown as sensitive and sympathetic to feminine needs. In general men are duplicitous. Each of Cecilia's guardians is proved inadequate as a protector. Self-seeking and with distorted values they deny Cecilia their support at crucial moments in her story. Even her own choice of lover is absent when she most depends on his support. The masquerade, held at the Harrel's house, is in itself an image of this male duplicity, an entertainment peopled by quick-change artistes, who hide their true characters behind the deceiving masks of a knight errant or a romantic hero. 'I protest', cries

Cecilia, to one such gallant, with a question that neatly encapsulates the theme of the book. 'I took you for my defender! Whence is it you are become my accuser?'

In the world of male hostility that Burney depicts, the issue of a name, around which the marriage theme manoeuvres, acquires symbolic value as the argument about Cecilia's name highlights the fundamental problem of the heroine's dilemma. If she retains her own name, Beverley, she also keeps her fortune and, in a society ruled by monetary qualifications, this equates with retaining her own identity. Delvile's family, with an inflated regard for their lineage, insist that this is out of the question. In begging Cecilia to renounce her relationship with Mortimer, Mrs Delvile pleads with her, 'in the name of Mr. Delvile, and in the name of our whole family, a family as ancient as it is honourable, and as honourable as it is ancient' explicitly invoking the power of heritage. The Delviles gain their distinction from historical antecedents, not from personal merit, and it is this that Cecilia's individualism must fight. As in Burney's other novels, the idea of the heroine's name is used to define her hold on her sense of self. Evelina has no name of her own until the final chapter of the book, when she receives two in quick succession, each demarcating a male appropriation. Belmont is her father's name; Orville her husband's, phonologically close to her guardian's choice, Anville, and suggestive of similar values. In *The Wanderer*, Juliet deliberately conceals her true name. She is the Incognita and only her husband provides her with a social identity. Without a name, she is abused and humiliated by a social hierarchy which is reliant on the power of inherited authority. But it is in *Cecilia* that the plot hinges on this issue and Burney makes it illustrate women's helplessness in the face of tradition and their tenuous hold on an independent identity.

Money, marriage and personality are thus intertwined in a complex thematic relationship that anticipates not only the novels of Fanny Burney's immediate successors but almost all novels by women written in the nineteenth century as well. In seeking freedom, Cecilia learns that to remain single is not the simple matter she expected 'You can do nothing at all without being married', the frivolous but street-wise Lady Honoria advises her. 'A single woman is a thousand times more shackled than a wife; for she is accountable to everybody; and a wife, you know, has nothing to do but just to manage her husband.'

It is Cecilia's responsible desire to be independent which singles her out from other fictional heroines of the period and from most of the eighteenth-century models of womanly perfection. Unlike these figures, and unlike Evelina, Cecilia is no ingenue but intelligent, confident and resourceful. Richardson's Clarissa is her main literary ancestor. Finding, even from the beginning of the novel, that others' opinions are not necessarily reliable, she disregards male advice when it conflicts with her own discriminating view. Social errors do not dismay her: the discovery that she has committed a faux pas in failing to return the visit of a young lady she has recently met only confirms her diagnosis that fashionable manners are ridiculous; certainly they form no ogre. Assured but not complacent in her opinions and poised in her behaviour, she is not intimidated by society but judgemental. Her lesson is therefore at once harsher and more complex than Evelina's for she has to learn not about conduct like her predecessor, nor about self-enlightenment like the Jane Austen and George Eliot women who succeeded her but about self-protection. In her confrontation with London, Cecilia discovers the false nature of civilised society and seeks a mechanism for adapting herself to its shallowness, hoping to create a meaningful existence in this barren environment according to her own sense of personal priorities. Her advice to Mrs Harrel about her slavish addiction to extravagance illustrates the moral dimension with which Burney invests self-reliance. 'Were it not better', Cecilia warns her friend, 'to think less of *other people* and more of *yourself*? to consult your own fortune, and your own situation in life, instead of being blindly guided by *other people*?' For her, personal integrity is at a premium and the tension between private and public codes of living is what Burney is intent on exposing. She does, however, make it abundantly clear that Cecilia's intellectual independence is a luxury, reliant on her independent means, and it is a commodity that women such as Henrietta Belfield cannot afford. *Cecilia* is a book which deals fundamentally with compromise, the lesson that Burney herself was in the painful process of learning as she was writing it.

Unlike her fictional contemporaries, Cecilia essentially is a rationalist, not a heroine of sensibility. When Harrel's suicide is discovered, it is her decision and firmness which come to the rescue. In a scene which is a precursor of Anne Elliot's experience on the Cobb in *Persuasion*, she retains her senses when others faint and, while motivated by compassion, her main efforts are directed towards immediate practicalities, such as finding a doctor, moving the body, consoling the widow. Similarly, her assistance to the bereaved Hill family concerns medical treatment, clothes for the children and business advice for the incompetent wife left behind with inadequate provision. Burney's view here is sharply anti-sentimental. The emotional response to the affecting aspects of the situations takes second place to coping with the primary realistic problems the situations produce.

The impression of women's education given in the novel informs this concept of character. This was a subject which Burney was to develop with a great deal more intensity in her next novel, *Camilla*, but she makes it apparent even here that the education of girls should contain a degree of intellectual rigour beyond what was normally deemed acceptable for elegant young women of the day. Burney is scathing in her portrait of Mr Delvile, the repository of patriarchal attitudes, who is convinced that 'the *Spectator*, *Tatler* & *Guardian* would make library sufficient for any female in the kingdom, nor do I think it like a gentlewoman to have more.' Aghast at Cecilia's keen appetite for literature (although Burney is perhaps deliberately coy about the specifics of her reading), he counsels her 'to remember that a lady, whether so called from birth or only from fortune, should never degrade herself by being put on a level with writers and that sort of people.' The popular feeling that, for women, breeding and scholarship were incompatible is shot down by the deliciousness of Burney's satire. She ironically condemns those men who require nothing more of a single woman than that 'she can dance a minuet or play upon the harpsichord' and her skittish, fashionable Lady Honoria supports the idea that, on a young lady of rank, study makes exorbitant demands for 'it's mighty well for children, but really, after sixteen, and when one is come out, one had quite fatigue enough in dressing and going to public places and ordering new things, without all that torment of first and second position, and E upon the first line and F upon the first space!'

Burney's attack on ignorance and her selection of a heroine who is both animated and reflective, gains extra significance in the context of the contemporary debate about women's abilities and the appropriateness of different educational methods. Some forty years earlier, Eliza Haywood had suggested that women be taught mathematics, philosophy, history and geography, for 'it is entirely owing to a narrow education that we either give our husbands room to find fault with our Conduct, or that we have leisure to pry too scrutinously into theirs.'[4] But Cecilia's education is designed not just to equip her for marriage but to supply her with intellectual resources that will provide her with permanent personal satisfaction. And this idea is supported by the presentation of Mrs Delvile, Cecilia's friend, as a woman who is literate, thoughtful and critical. Mrs Delvile isolates herself from modish society, is openly dismissive of gossip

and welcomes Cecilia's mental precision and clarity.
Notwithstanding her faults (she is proud and sardonic),
Cecilia finds her company stimulating and happily spends
hours with her. Bound in an emotionally sterile marriage,
Mrs Delvile responds to Cecilia's warmth and a deep mutual
friendship develops. Mrs Delvile is in fact a tantalising
character, suggestive of thwarted ideals but capable too of
behaving according to comic stereotype, the classic
obstructive parent. Burney's intention with Mrs Delvile, 'to
blend upon paper, as I have frequently seen blended in life,
noble and rare qualities with striking and incurable defects',
substantiates her rejection of a conventional romantic ideal
and this is strengthened further by the choice of Henrietta
Belfield as a secondary character. Intuitive, emotional and
dreamy, Henrietta contains many of the 'feminine' qualities
normally found in fictional heroines of the time. But while
Cecilia finds her warm and engaging, her extreme sensitivity
is shown by Burney to be a liability rather than an asset. The
features she exemplifies are rather like those of Frances
Brooke's Lady Julia Mandeville (1763), whose mind is
'adorned, not warped by education, it is just what her
appearance promises; artless, gentle, timid, soft, sincere,
compassionate; awake to all the first impressions of
tenderness and melting with pity for every human woe.'[5] The
portraits of Mrs Delvile and Henrietta together illuminate
Burney's slant on the two popular theories of the day about
women's nature that combine in the characterisation of
Cecilia. The consequent emergence of a feeling heroine of
initiative and common sense in a world where the odds are
stacked against her was to pave the way for the release of
similarly spirited creations by other women writers.

Charlotte Smith's novels, chasing on *Cecilia's* heels,
demonstrate this debt to Fanny Burney. The title character
in *Emmeline* (1788) defies the sacred infallibility of
aristocratic opinion by speaking her own mind and quite
shocks the hidebound Lord Montreville who is outraged that

'a little weak girl should pretend to a sense of rectitude and a force of understanding greater than his own'.[6] Like Burney's women, Emmeline's moral sensibility is presented as superior to the values imposed upon her by an uncaring society which is casually prepared to compromise her reputation. Less radical in her conception than Cecilia, she conforms more to the model of the advanced young lady proposed by the educator and critic, Mrs Barbauld, who believed that 'every woman should consider herself as sustaining the general character of a rational being', but that 'in no subject is she required to be deep, – of none ought she to be ignorant'.[7] Emmeline, knowledgeable and accomplished, is also for most of the time silent and modest, well aware that as Mrs Barbauld admitted, 'the thefts of knowledge in our sex are only connived at while carefully concealed, and if displayed, punished with disgrace.' With this in mind, most women novelists in the past had permitted only their minor characters the luxury of an independent spirit. Frances Brooke's witty Arabella Fermor appears as a foil to the beautiful and conventional heroine of *Lady Emily Montague* (1769). Lively and articulate, she is allowed by her creator to regret that 'every possible means is used, even from infancy, to soften the minds of women, and to harden those of men'[8] but she is kept firmly to the sidelines of the main action. Similarly, the sophisticated Lady Anne Wilmot, in Brooke's *Lady Julia Mandeville*, emerges in her supporting role as the most likeable and alert character the novel has to offer, cool and cynical in her attitude towards the opposite sex. But it was really only towards the end of the century that such women began to be given centre stage. Miss Milner, the dynamic heroine of the first half of Elizabeth Inchbald's *A Simple Story* (1791), carries the novel's entire weight of sympathy. A passionate being, she actively resists the dictatorial attempts of her stuffy guardian to control her. Asserting her right to act as she pleases, she flaunts her bravado and disobeys his commands so seductively that,

despite his disapproval of her behaviour, her guardian falls in
love with her and becomes her husband. Such an explicit
meshing of the twin male roles of authority and romance
accentuates the problem of women's perception of men that
we find again and again in novels of this period. The fact that
Miss Milner is punished for her rebelliousness and the
heroine of the second part of the book, her daughter, is mild
and dutiful in no way detracts from the challenge to
establishment values that the book encodes.

However, despite the creation of a heroine whose stature is
of a different order from her predecessors, Burney's *Cecilia*,
in its overall concept, still suggests an uneasy tension
between realistic and romantic elements. Cecilia herself,
offset by the rationalism and sentimentalism of Mrs Delvile
and Henrietta respectively, veers from being a fully rounded
character to a symbolic figure. The mad scenes at the end of
the novel when, distracted and abandoned, she becomes
delirious provide a sharp contrast with the early episodes of
the book. The change from the level-headed young woman
we have been encouraged to identify with, to the
melodramatic, stylised being she becomes, takes place in a
setting that highlights the intensity of the transformation.
The final chapters offer powerful images of Cecilia, Clarissa-
like, lost in London, surrounded by a hostile mob,
imprisoned in a strange uncomfortable house, ill and
helpless. The freedom that she has sought so determinedly
throughout the preceding volumes is at last proved an
illusory goal and her real powerlessness is laid bare in the
vividly pictorial quality of her suffering. Physically she
undergoes an alteration so startling that even her closest
friends have difficulty recognising her. 'Is *This* she herself! –
can *This* be Cecilia!' cries Albany, horror-struck at seeing
his original prophecy fulfilled in such graphic detail.

What is so frightening to Cecilia as, 'breathless with
vehemence and terror', she uselessly tries to reason with the
mob that takes her for an escaped lunatic is the stark evidence

of the failure of her own rationalism. Earlier she had increasingly suspected that the system that entraps her is beyond logic. Now these suspicions are concentrated in a series of rapid developments that act in the novel as a dramatic metaphor of women's weakness. Cecilia has tried to resist all along the patriarchal model of womanly behaviour but these concluding scenes show her reduced to the passive, fragile and raving figure that men expect women to be. Delvile sees her 'feeble, shaking, leaning upon one person, and half carried by another!' and she graduates through a process of accommodation to her state, as 'wholly insensible but perfectly quiet; she seemed to distinguish nothing, and neither spoke nor moved'. Eventually her recovery from illness and the return to full recollection and consciousness leave her 'faint and weak, and contentedly silent, to avoid the effort of speaking'. The metamorphosis is complete.

The very ending of *Cecilia* emphasises both the schematic approach to the work that Burney adopted and the message of compromise that the technique involves. The happy ending of marriage bows conventionally in the direction of the romance tradition but Burney imparts a cynical note to this vision of contentment in her closing maxims. Cecilia's happiness is human 'and as such imperfect', and the concluding words of the book undermine the credibility of romance as a solution.

> Rationally, however, she surveyed the world at large, and finding that of the few who had any happiness, there were none without some misery, she checked the rising sigh of repining mortality, and, grateful with general felicity, bore partial evil with chearfullest resignation.

'Resignation' is, significantly, the note on which the novel ends. Cecilia's future has been purchased at a price.

5 Camilla

From the outset, Fanny Burney visualised *Camilla* as being different from her other books because it would be a 'concord'. After a fourteen-year absence from the literary scene, she was determined to safeguard her reputation as a novelist of distinction. She wanted her new work to attain a high level of both artistic and moral seriousness, for her recent change of status to wife and mother would permit her no frivolity. She thought carefully about her master plan and confided to her father that 'I do not like calling it a Novel; it gives so simply the notion of a mere love story that I recoil a little from it. I mean it to be sketches of Characters and Morals put in action, not a Romance.' The gravity of tone was to be matched by the book's design, for she wanted it to be 'of the same species as *Evelina* and *Cecilia*; new modified in being more multifarious . . . but all wove into one . . . for so far is the work from consisting of detached stories that there is not, literally, one Episode in the whole Plan.' This was to be a consciously structured and integrated composition but Burney's lofty intentions could not conceal her real motives for returning to writing; her urgent need for funds.

This in itself suggests something about the way in which the position of women writers had changed since *Evelina* was secretively allowed to make its entrance into the world. Since 1780, the number of published works by female authors had been growing year by year, as novels, moral tales, reviews, historical treatises and educational tracts poured from female pens. Many received favourable critical notice and, by the end of the century, attitudes towards literate women were no longer as uniformly hostile or suspicious as they had been thirty years earlier. Between the appearance of *Evelina* and *Camilla* nearly two hundred novels were published by women under their own names and even though there was still a sprinkling which coyly announced the author as 'a lady', anonymity was no longer a prerequisite for female writers. In such a climate Mme D'Arblay, as she now was, was not ashamed to capitalise on her juvenile successes and a conscious professionalism informs *Camilla*. With its carefully wrought and competently handled material it has no flavour of the work of a clever amateur. Solidly announcing its public nature throughout, the book is perhaps deadened by the sometimes naked appeal to popular taste but Burney, responsible now for her own and her family's livelihood, had come to recognise the vital necessity of economic reward. A book was a marketable commodity and with this in mind, in consultation with her family, she decided that her most beneficial move would be to publish her new work by subscription. Aware that her first publishers had profited by her admitted commercial inexperience, she was insistent that this time no-one should take advantage of her, and working with her brothers as mediators, she shopped around industriously for the most lucrative offer she could attract.

A nervousness about literary quality, however, still plagued her and she was like a child in her desperation for the approval of those she revered. 'I will make the work the best I can, my dearest Father', she promised, painfully anxious as always about her own shortcomings. 'I will be neither indolent, nor negligent, nor avaricious. I can never half answer the expectations that seem excited! I must try to forget them or I shall be in a continuous quivering.' But to forget the public gaze was impossible. As in the past she worked furiously to meet the deadline advertised by her booksellers, 1 July 1796, her adoring husband doing his best to help her by acting as copyist, unwittingly scattering the transcript with grammatical inaccuracies as he wrote.

In spite of its grandiose aspirations and the dedication to the Queen, meant to reinforce its respectability and retain Royal approval (and the pension that went with it), *Camilla* was panned by the critics. 'Many blemishes may be found', noted the *British Critic*, '. . . transgressions against grammar . . . Gallicisms . . . the story is doubtless spun out to an immoderate length'.[1] Burney took the criticisms to heart and was at first bitterly hurt by what she interpreted as malicious personal attacks but her interest in the marketplace soon reasserted itself and here she was not disappointed. *Camilla* did astonishingly well, the sales exceeding Fanny's wildest expectations. After a bare three months, only 500 copies remained out of the original printing of 4000 and the D'Arblays were able to build and furnish their own home on the proceeds. Typically, Fanny had not learned as much as she thought about the ways of the commercial world and in their innocence the couple failed to appreciate the legal niceties of property speculation. When their leasehold land was later sold, their home, the precious *Camilla Cottage*, had to be abandoned.

Despite her initial dismay at *Camilla*'s reception, Fanny Burney was now sufficiently experienced to be able to balance the conflicting claims of popular and critical rewards with a somewhat jaundiced eye. A few months after the book's appearance, she was able to comment that both 'Politics and Novels will be judged by the various multitude not the fastidious few . . . and want no recommendation for being handed about but that of being New'. It was a pity that such asperity did not infiltrate the text more pervasively, for more than any other of her novels, *Camilla* panders to the contemporary vogue for moral fable and in so doing exhibits a sense of deep unease as Burney attempts to accommodate her private thoughts to public tastes.

Always self-aware, Fanny Burney had become since her marriage more sensitive than ever to what she felt ought to be her new persona. Inevitably, her perspective on events had altered a great deal since she wrote her youthful high-spirited comedies. With an economic clear-sightedness, she also knew that she needed to bow to her public in order to boost sales figures. What she perhaps failed to take into account was the validity of her personal vision of uncertainty to a culture that was itself in the process of transition. In attempting to cater to the demands of a mass audience, she tried to conceal her own anxieties about conformism and this lack of confidence had a stultifying effect. Still hoping to be a mid-stream follower, rather than a leader, of intellectual fashion, she struggled to muffle her original voice beneath an adopted prosy tone and the novel contains laborious passages when she monotonously lectures her readers. The story line is almost non-existent as the action is largely subordinated to the didactic purpose. Although we can still see the Burney magic delighting in the oddities of comic personalities, she seemed to be unable to make up her mind whether her characters should be familiar representations of moral stereotypes, such as 'the dandy', 'the wastrel' or 'the old maid', or should have more individuality and this sort of technical inconsistency is some reflection of the uncertainties which lie behind the impulses of the novel.

Written during a period when Romanticism was gaining a hold over the minds and imaginations of an entire generation, *Camilla* discloses most provocatively the contradictions of its antecedents. It is set for the most part in the country and the impact of early Romantic leanings is evident in the descriptions of the picturesque rural landscape, the charm exerted by rustic characters, the uncontestable attractions of the sentimental poet, Melmond, and the beauty of his languid sister, Mrs Berlinton. Although by the end of the novel, Burney has subjected the values of sensibility to a rigorous moral scrutiny (and found them wanting), the sympathies of the text are in fact ambiguous. This ambiguity can be detected in the choice and management of subject matter which develops the theme of female initiation from her previous two novels. In extending her range of vision to encompass a wider field – a whole family is the focus of attention here not just a single heroine – Burney subscribes to the widespread current interest in childhood and adolescent development. This was not an entirely new phenomenon. The popularity of educational guides and conduct books was at its height in the years surrounding the turn of the century. The moral works of Dr Gregory, Mrs Chapone, Lord Halifax, Dr Gisborne, Mrs More and Mrs Palmer were all best sellers during the period 1770–1800, together with several famous collections of sermons which offered systematic advice on inculcating correct codes of behaviour in young people. Always suspicious of deviance, Fanny Burney recommended a regular annual dose of Mrs Chapone's medicinal *Letters on the Improvement of the Mind* to her great nieces and when her son Alex was growing up she worried constantly about his waywardness and his predilection for chess rather than the rigour of study.

But an alternative and more radical philosophy was gaining credence. Jean-Jacques Rousseau's autobiographical the *Confessions* had been published in English in 1783, generating a degree of excitement among writers who responded with enthusiasm to the subjective record of personal growth as an active process. This stimulating approach to character formation as dynamic and fluid opened up a new perspective on the concept of autobiography, a technique that was already deeply interwoven with the method of female fiction. As the activities of childhood were perceived as carrying new significance, the connections between early experience and the development of the later personality were examined in a number of novels, especially in those by women, traditional specialists in the art of child rearing. Many of these fictions, tentative in their assertions, appeared finally to endorse the more conservative aspects of educational theory but the very choice of a biographical format had by the latter years of the century taken on new meaning. So when Mrs Inchbald, a great admirer of Rousseau, explored the tensions between passion and principle in *A Simple Story*, she ascribed her heroine's caprice to her lack of A PROPER EDUCATION.[2] Although there is no mention in her journals that she was familiar with the *Confessions*, Burney had certainly read Rousseau's *Emile*, a novel which advocated a philosophy of individual development based on a freedom from rigid ethical codes. Growing up was no longer to be dismissed as an unfortunate but easily forgotten stage in human experience. It was a serious matter, and Burney was profoundly disturbed by the implications of the topical arguments raging around the whole subject of social education.

Camilla's subtitle is *A Picture of Youth*. It is Burney's contribution to the lively contemporary debate on the enormously complex topic of human development, as it concentrates on the effects of upbringing on a group of children who are subjected to a variety of environmental influences. Burney needed the wider stage in order to indicate the complicated nature of the issues involved and her presentation of behavioural patterns is indeed the 'concord' that she claimed. It is organised as an enquiry into the competing claims of nature and discipline and all the youthful characters offer modifications of this theme. The Tyrold children live close to their rich bachelor uncle, Sir Hugh, a well meaning bumbler, who interferes with their lives with some disastrous results. They grow up side by side with his wards, their spoiled cousins Indiana and Clermont Lynmere, and a wealthy neighbour, a ward of their father's, Edgar Mandelbert. In focusing on the children, Burney does not neglect the adults in this community, who are seen in their roles as bemused guides and preceptors. Sir Hugh, the governess Miss Margland, the tutors Dr Orkborne and Dr Marchmont and the virtuous and earnest Tyrold parents comprise a thorough investigation into the effects of liberalism and authoritarianism, as it is their often mistaken attitudes which are shown to result in the problems of the young.

While obviously interested in the general premises of educational philosophy, – we find for instance a textbook example of two boys whose individual natures triumph over their identical backgrounds – Burney reserves special attention for the discussion of the management of girls. By singling out her heroine, Camilla Tyrold, for sustained analysis, she combines the traditional maxims of the conduct guides of the age, with the more flexible and forward looking insights into the ideas surrounding emotional and moral growth. Camilla is one of those fully-rounded and imperfect heroines who are so familiar to the post-Jane Austen reader but who stood out as exceptional among the pale and passive dummies who were her fictional contemporaries. Warm-hearted, sensitive and impulsive, like Marianne Dashwood, she is swayed by her immediate impressions and frequently suffers accordingly. Her mentors counsel her severely against emotional extravagance – 'It is time to conquer this impetuous sensibility', her level-headed mother admonishes her – but Camilla cannot be taken simply as a warning against the dangers of sentimentalism, for her feeling heart forms one of her major assets. At the centre of the novel's ambivalence, she charms in spite of, or because of, her defects. No staid moral paragon, she is deliberately conceived as a flawed character, an active high-spirited girl, whose faults are the natural ones of inexperience and whose freshness and spontaneity are genuine gifts. She is a human, not an artificial, creation, although by the end of the novel her sparkle has been dimmed considerably as she is beaten by experience into an acceptable conformist specimen. With an innate sense of personal integrity, her errors stem only from a lack of circumspection and what she has to acquire is a more subtle sense of social awareness than her parents can instil into her. Doctrine, Burney suggests, cannot take the place of experiential learning.

The first volume of *Camilla* is concerned with childhood episodes and childish behaviour is shown to reveal the germs of the adult personality. Burney's children, set within a clear ethical framework, are commended or reproved for their actions, always with a purposeful eye on their emergence as adolescents and mature adults. The plot is minimal. As Burney had been keen to point out to her father, this is a 'work' rather than a novel. But the book is much more than an elaborate guide to juvenile conduct. It provides a searching and often sceptical look at the bases of current educational theory and practice, particularly for young women, and behind the orthodox linkage of manners and morals lies a subtext that is often deeply critical of the training offered to girls to equip them for the rigours of the world they must encounter.

'It is necessary for you to be perfect in the *first four rules of Arithmetic*; more you can never have occasion for, and the mind should not be burdened with needless application',[3] wrote Lady Sarah Pennington in *An Unfortunate Mother's Advice to her Absent Daughters*. This was a tract so popular that it was still considered pertinent reading for young ladies in 1825, when it was republished more than fifty years after its first appearance. In *Camilla*, the mean-minded governess, Miss Margland, is made the ironic mouthpiece for such a view, nervous that her charge, the glorious Indiana, who is in serious training to be a coquette, will injure her looks with too much reading. The perfect weapon for Burney's satire, narrow, ignorant and egoistic herself, Miss Margland passes on these qualities to her pupil, convinced that scholarship in a woman is a positive obstacle to her future success, for 'what gentleman will you ever find that will bear with a learned wife?' Moderation, she pleads, is essential, 'a little music, a little drawing, a little dancing; which should all be but slightly pursued, to distinguish a lady of fashion from an artist'. The knife is surely twisted with the final phrase. Originality must be suppressed in this philistine, patriarchal

society. Indiana's lack of interest in study and her cultivation
of the traditional female accomplishments of weeping and
pouting are lampooned by Burney, whose women in this
novel are frequently more astute and intellectually agile than
her men. Fanny Burney never denies girls native mental
ability. Indiana is depicted as lazy rather than dim-witted.
She is carefully balanced by the portrayal of her cousin,
Eugenia, and together the two form an illustration of
Burney's thesis on women and education.

Hampered by physical defects, after a tragic accident when
she was eight years old, and consequently bereft of the more
active pastimes of childhood, Eugenia eagerly embraces the
classical curriculum offered her. Her progress is rapid and
she effortlessly outstrips her brother, her uncle and her
cousin Clermont, a public school product, becoming
knowledgeable and thoughtful without any hint of pedantry.
Her achievements, however, are sharply contrasted with her
appearance; for her deformities make her into a laughing
stock when she ventures into public and her academic
accomplishments add to her reputation as an eccentric for
'some imagined her studies had stunted her growth; and all
were convinced her education had made her such a fright'.
When rumour spreads that she is an heiress, she is abducted
by an unscrupulous fortune-hunter, who imprisons her and
maltreats her in a manner reminiscent of the worst excesses of
Gothicism. Eugenia's fate demonstrates the reductive power
of social values. What use are her scholarly advantages in a
world where women are judged according to narrow
standards of marketability and marriage is the only viable
career on offer? Tuition in self-protection is what is needed
but Eugenia's seclusion from society has made her naive,
idealistic and thus easy prey. Learning, Burney stresses
regretfully, is no substitute for worldly awareness and those
responsible for adolescent guidance must steer a delicate path
between the two.

Precisely how delicate is indicated in the chapter Burney

devotes to Mr Tyrold's sermon to Camilla on the subject of
women's education. This was a section of the book which
received widespread critical acclaim – 'so large and lustrous a
brilliant'[4] the *Monthly Review* called it – for its edifying
nature and which was added as a postscript to the 1809
reissue of Dr Gregory's *Legacy*. Mr Tyrold's refusal to enter
into the controversy over male and female roles is
symptomatic of Burney's own pragmatic stance. 'There
cannot in nature, in theory, even in common sense be a doubt
of their equal right' to freedom of choice, he admits, but the
tenor of his advice is directed towards an acceptance of the
limited options available. In recognising the potential
dangers of women's lives, he sees in conformism and
submission their best chance of survival. His advocacy of
patience, self-control, good-sense, delicacy and moral
discrimination is not intended to be an unthinking repetition
of the standard precepts of the conduct books but rather a
considered view that only these qualities hold the key to
female salvation. As Mr Tyrold clarifies the constraints on
women's roles, he suggests the indeterminacies and perils
that confront women at all stages of their lives. It is an
impossible task for parents to educate their daughters, he
explains, because 'the temporal destiny of women is enwrapt
in still more impenetrable obscurity than that of man'. A
girl's future is an unknown quantity, more sinister than a
boy's because it is largely out of her control. As financial
dependants, choice and liberal sympathies are luxuries most
women cannot afford.

Radical or conservative in their bias, most thoughtful
women writers were fairly generally agreed about the
inadequacies of the current system of girls' education. Mary
Wollstonecraft and Hannah More, at opposite ends of the
political spectrum, shared with Burney the perception of
female repression. 'I must declare what I firmly believe',
asserted Wollstonecraft in *A Vindication of the Rights of
Women*, 'that all the writers who have written on the subject

of female education from Rousseau to Dr. Gregory, have
contributed to render women more artificial, weak
characters than they would otherwise have been.'[5] While in
her *Strictures on the Modern System of Female Education*,
Hannah More was just as positive. 'It is a singular injustice
which is often exercised towards women', she complained,
'first to give them a very defective education, and then to
expect from them the most undeviating purity of conduct'.[6]
Camilla takes up these points as key issues. It is the arbitrary
aspect of women's lives that Burney dramatises so
convincingly throughout the novel, in a series of incidents
that reinforce the view of women as victims of their culture.
It is a view which suggests an alternative perspective to the
apparent orthodoxy of the overriding moral doctrine the text
would appear to propose. The erratic nature of women's
social inheritance is powerfully demonstrated in the
haphazard way in which the foolish moneybags, Sir Hugh,
changes his will, disinheriting his nieces according to the
whim of the moment. Whether it be material or physical,
their legacy is unjust, as the fate of Eugenia most forcefully
illustrates. She is disfigured by the smallpox and then lamed
by a fall. Both afflictions result from her uncle's carelessness,
as she changes in a few hours from a normal healthy little girl
with a bright future ahead of her to a bizarre freak, a dramatic
casualty of masculine neglect.

Camilla herself is made into an unwitting target of gossip
and male suspicion and there are times in the novel when she
seems to mirror the plight of all women who fail to live up to
the impossible standards expected of them by men. Much of
the story concerns the development of her romance with the
Grandisonian boy-next-door hero, Edgar Mandelbert. Edgar
is in love with Camilla but he allows his ardour to be curbed
by the world-weary cavilling of the misogynist, Dr
Marchmont. With Marchmont's encouragement, Edgar
watches and judges Camilla. Her every move is scrutinised
and the possible interpretations of her most casual gesture

analysed exhaustively in order to assess her suitability as a wife. Male rationalism is all powerful and love is a reward that can be withheld at the slightest sign of female caprice. As Camilla moves from one rash action to another, followed by a strong dose of remorse at each stage, Edgar decides one minute to marry her, the next to discard her. The novel's progress provides an active demonstration of the tenets asserted by Evelina's watchdog, Mr Villars, that a woman's reputation is a priceless commodity as its loss, however innocent, can irrevocably damage her future prospects.

While the action would appear to support this philosophy wholeheartedly, from within the text, Burney provides a penetrating critique of her priggish hero through the comments of the lively and independent-minded Mrs Arlbery, the society hostess who fascinates Camilla. 'Mandelbert', she scathingly declares, 'is a creature whose whole composition is a pile of accumulated punctilios.' Her deflation of Edgar's rectitude, accomplished with charm and vitality, acts to undercut the values that he embodies and exposes the tension that exists in the novel between a surface conformism and an undercurrent that constantly questions and subverts. Mrs Arlbery, a character who muddies the definition of Burney's attitude considerably, bridges the gap between sympathy and judgement that our response to Mandelbert originally elicits and creates a positive counter to the moral authority that he and the Tyrold parents try to establish.

The more closely we read *Camilla*, the more apparent is the dissension from establishment values. Mrs Arlbery, attractive and witty, a woman whose own lifestyle forms a successful challenge to convention, is a character who helps sow the seeds of suspicion. Clearly, Burney found it difficult to present her in accordance with the prevailing fictional conventions. She is precisely the sort of woman that Burney admired in real life, combining an incisive intelligence with grace and vitality. But with its own reputation to protect, the

female fictional world was not yet ready to adopt such a
woman as its model and the imaginative sympathy invested
in her portrayal is at odds with the sententious moral opinion
of the novel, which is compelled to take a disapproving line
towards such flamboyant individualism. Mrs Arlbery's
cynicism about romance and marriage, however, is endorsed
in a variety of ways, as Burney questions quite trenchantly
the contemporary idea that marriage is a perfectly
satisfactory career for young women.

Fanny Burney herself, married at forty-one, had been
most reluctant to commit herself any earlier to a lifelong
union. In a letter to a friend, she described how 'I had never
made any vow against marriage, but I had LONG – LONG
been persuaded it was – for ME – a state of too much hazard
and too little promise, to draw me from my individual plans
and purposes.' Her recognition of the inevitable clash
between 'individual plans' and the lottery of amorous
fulfilment pervades *Camilla* as the realities of married life
are shown to be quite different from heady expectation.
Marchmont, a character of sober experience and not without
judgement, outlines the pressures placed on women to
marry.

> Ask half the married women in the nation how they
> became wives: they will tell you their friends urged them
> . . . that they had no other establishment in view . . . that
> nothing is so uncertain as the repetition of matrimonial
> powers in women . . . and that those who cannot solicit
> what they wish must accommodate themselves to what
> offers.

The awareness of female insecurity dominates Marchmont's
cutting vision of the sex. It is the fear of the future that results
in the compromise of most female lives and mingled with
Marchmont's contempt is Burney's sympathy for the
innocent and exaggerated reliance on youth and beauty as

natural advantages. Time and again she stresses the dual nature of these sought after feminine attributes. The qualities which secure male approval also put women at risk, as Camilla's frightening encounter with Lord Valhurst demonstrates. For the pretty but unprotected girl, masculine attention is difficult to handle, with seduction and ruin a real and hazardous alternative to honourable marriage and lifelong security. Burney's greatest anger, however, is reserved for the conditions which have fostered such an iniquitous system.

The protest against the essential helplessness of women's predicament accelerates with the portrayal of Miss Dennel, an adolescent scarcely out of the schoolroom, who longs to be married so as to escape the prison of her father's house. Her hope that marriage will equip her magically with independence, authority and social stature is proved to be sadly illusory and she finds herself, at fifteen, bitterly resentful of the trick that society has played upon her.

> She had not, she said, half so much liberty as when she lived with her Papa, and heartily repented marrying and wished she had never thought of it. The servants were always teazing her for orders and directions; everything that went wrong, it was always she who was asked why it was not right . . . if she wanted to do something she liked, he said she had better let it alone; and in fine her violent desire for this state of freedom ended in conceiving it a state of bondage; she found *her own house* the house of which she must take the charge; being *her own mistress* having the burthen of superintending a whole family; and being *married*, becoming the property of another, to whom she made over a legal right to treat her just as he pleased.

Burney's tone changes in this passage from one of light-hearted comic exposure of Miss Dennel's youthful irresponsibility to a harsher note, as the attack mounts on the

society which pressurises young girls into marriage with false
expectations. Unprepared for what she might find, Miss
Dennel moves from one sort of servitude to another, with no
opportunity to realise her identity as an individual. She forms
a frightening exemplar of the truth of Mrs Arlbery's acid
prophecy of the certain failure of wedded bliss.

> A man looks enchanted while his beautiful young bride
> talks nonsense; it comes prettily from her ruby lips, and
> she blushes and dimples with such lovely attractions while
> she utters it . . . but he has ample turns for looking like a
> fool himself, when youth and beauty take flight, and when
> his ugly old wife exposes her ignorance or folly at every
> word.

Not a very inviting prospect – and interestingly anticipating
Jane Austen's Mr and Mrs Bennet – but Miss Dennel's future
cannot hold out any sounder possibilities of happiness. It is a
savage indictment of the institution on which most women's
livelihood depends but the alternatives that the system
contains are pronounced equally bleak.

Burney certainly furnishes no solution in her presentation
of the single life. Two spinsters in the novel, Miss Margland
and Mrs Mittin (the latter having taken the title *Mrs* to avoid
humiliation), demonstrate the ignominy of lonely, penurious
lives. Neither has the resources, either personal or financial,
to find fulfilment, as neglected by the social groups they
aspire to, they are shown to be constantly eager for notice and
dependent on patronage. Only men can provide the social
cachet they need for self-respect. Miss Margland, comic but
pathetic, tries desperately to make a beau out of the unlikely
pedant, Dr Orkborne, for even though she had not 'the most
remote hope of inspiring him to any gallantry: but still he was
a man, and she thought it a mark of consequence to have one
in her train.'

In her thoughts on marriage, it would appear that Fanny

Burney has in mind an ultimate ideal, where mutual respect and friendly companionship are seen as essential constituents. The eventual unions of Camilla, and her sisters, Lavinia and Eugenia, satisfy these criteria of personal and social qualifications, where individual suitability is backed up by economic considerations. But none of this is shown to be at all inevitable. Camilla gains the love of Edgar, partly because she learns to conform to the model he requires but also because of a series of fortuitous circumstances which bring him to her side when it seems that all hope is lost. The denouement of the novel in fact confirms the emphasis on chance as a dominant factor in female experience. Virtue on its own is ineffective in securing a good husband. Luck too must play its part and Burney provides in *Camilla* some devastating examples of less fortunate alliances than the Tyrold sisters manage to realise.

Eugenia's first marriage is a travesty of a Richardsonian plot. Doomed to be a victim, she is kidnapped by a manic villain, intent on possessing her money, who veers between protestations of love and acts of brutality and who creates a horrific picture of cruelty and deceit. The wedding ceremony, where Eugenia 'uttered not one word; she was passive, scared and scarce alive, but resisted not the eventful ring with which he encircled her finger' communicates a powerful metaphor of the triumph of masculine force and its paralytic effects. The history of Mrs Berlinton, compelled by her family to make a loveless match with an old, sick husband, who 'supposed he had engaged for life a fair nurse to his infirmities' is only a sample of what Burney acknowledges to be common practice. 'The ill fate of such unequal alliances is almost daily exemplified in life', she comments sourly, as the canvas of *Camilla* gradually fills with images of women disposed of by social formulae.

Any attempt to defy custom and escape the restrictive and weakening net of society is treated most diffidently by Burney. Mrs Berlinton leaves her husband and tries to launch her own establishment. A warm, generous and sensitive woman, she engages our interest and Camilla's loyalty in much the same way as Mrs Arlbery but Burney is not prepared to endorse these qualities or her stand for independence indiscriminately and insists on making her morally fallible. Mrs Berlinton's defective education (which apparently consisted mostly of reading novels of the wrong type) has resulted in a want of solid principle, which in turn leads her into a reprehensible way of life in which flirtation and gambling are central diversions. Like Mrs Arlbery, Mrs Berlinton's rebelliousness can only invite tantalising hints of the true direction of Burney's sympathies, for like the other women, conformism is recommended as her route to salvation.

The relationship of the Tyrold parents is perhaps held up as the best model of a marriage the novel can supply but even this is imperfect. Despite the indubitable mutual respect and affection between the couple, there is serious division. At the beginning of the book, when Sir Hugh wants Camilla to leave her home and be brought up in his care, Mrs Tyrold acquiesces only with the greatest reluctance, submitting to her husband's judgement, in spite of her own shrewder misgivings. How far does Burney sanction such a paragon of wifely obedience? Mrs Tyrold yields because 'she never resisted a remonstrance of her husband: and as her sense of duty impelled her also never to murmur, she returned to her own room, to conceal with how ill a grace she complied'. Silence and compromise fall to women's lot but had she only protested, her daughters might have been spared their future calamities. That their mother's first opinion of Sir Hugh is proved right is no great consolation in the face of Eugenia's and Camilla's sufferings.

By the end of the novel, Burney has returned to her distanced pedagogic position, drawing stringent moral conclusions from her interwoven strands. The miscreants are punished; the deviants conform and the innocent find happiness. This tidy arrangement, however, is artificial and unsatisfying for the main impression left by the novel is one of women hounded by unattainable goals of perfection, their security purchased only with the loss of their individuality.

This sort of discrepancy was to be exploited with much more poignant ironic weight by Jane Austen, one of the original subscribers to *Camilla* and Burney's literary heir in so many ways. Of all Burney's novels *Camilla* is perhaps the one which exerted the greatest influence on her successor, the resemblances to *Mansfield Park* being particularly striking. 'Let other pens dwell on guilt and misery' begins Austen's coda, as she conveniently dismisses in Burneyesque fashion the sufferings of her characters, including the sustained portrayal of the loneliness and neglect of Fanny Price, the central and most pervasive image of the novel. Numerous parallels can be drawn between the two books, with their emphasis on the family situation, their analyses of moral education and their theme of spiritual inheritance. The sober Edgar Mandelbert closely anticipates Edmund Bertram, the wild Lionel Tyrold is a precursor of Tom Bertram and the shallow Indiana looks forward to Maria Bertram, shut up for her final purgatory with the one who has spoiled her, the spiteful and parsimonious Mrs Norris, a more waspish version of Miss Margland. Those amoral sophisticates, the Crawfords, have their roots in Mrs Arlbery and her worldly companion, Sir Sedley Clarendel, as figures who seductively introduce the glamour of metropolitan style to the relatively secluded world of the country estate. In the placing and measuring of different codes of living, Burney does not have the artistic economy of Austen, nor her comic subtlety but the similarities between the two writers go way beyond the noting of narrative details. In *Camilla*, Burney initiates a mode of expression where the tension between conformist text and mutinous subtext shows how women were finding ways of employing traditional and acceptable forms of writing for their own purposes. It was a mode which

Austen took up and became an expert in and which in turn was crucial in determining the approaches of so many women writers of the nineteenth century. When Virginia Woolf announced that Jane Austen should have laid a wreath on the grave of Fanny Burney, it may well have been of *Camilla* that she was thinking.

6 The Wanderer

The Wanderer is at once Fanny Burney's dullest and her most exciting novel. 'If we had not been assured in the title page that this work had been produced by the same pen as *Cecilia*', yawned the *Quarterly Review* of 1814, 'we should have pronounced Madame D'Arblay to be a feeble imitator of the style and manner of Miss Burney. . . . 'Even in her best days Madame D'Arblay's style had a predisposition to self-imitation and tautology', it relentlessly continued, 'but in *The Wanderer* there is no splendour, no source of delight to dazzle criticism and beguile attention from a defect which has increased in size and deformity exactly in the same degree that the beauties have vanished.'[1] Sadly, we are forced to agree. Aspects of the novel are indeed quite awful: the style is a sort of laborious sub-Johnsonese; the plot is contrived beyond the bounds of plausibility; the main character is a colourless replica of a human being. Yet, surprisingly, it is also in this last novel, written over a period spanning fifteen years, that Burney most boldly confronts issues which had been lurking tremulously close to the surface of her previous works but which had never before dared to emerge outright. The novel's subtitle comes clean at once. *Female Difficulties* is the acknowledged subject and Burney simultaneously liberates her topic from the conduct guide stable and moves explicitly into the provocative minefield of sexual politics.

For undoubtedly this is a political novel, in more ways than one, and it carries a sombre message. Gone are the giggles of amusement at the foibles of quirky individuals; gone are the sprightly vignettes. In their place are savage portraits of overbearing matrons and offensively pushy young men, unalleviated by comic absurdity. Burney, publishing again after nearly twenty years, was understandably nervous about her faithful fans' reaction to her change of tone and subject for the massive advance publicity had blazoned the work as a sparkling French version of the comedy of manners à la *Evelina*. In a lengthy preface, dedicated to her father, she tried to forestall criticism that the book contained 'materials for political controversy; or fresh food for national animosity'. The novel, she disarmingly claimed, is 'simply a work of invention and observation'. How could she have thought to get away with it so easily? Despite its decorous surface, the text positively crackles with seditious opinions.

Having lived abroad for ten years, comfortably assimilated into French culture, Burney's view of English life had acquired the bitter edge of distance and from start to finish the narrative is coloured by her sharpened perception of England as an alien place. In *The Wanderer* her native land takes on the stamp of a foreign country, a country where bigotry, insularity and callousness are seen as the salient national characteristics. No longer are the upper social echelons of the British bourgeoisie presented as glamorous or even attractive havens for young women to aspire to. Juliet Granville, the Wanderer of the title, is no naive maiden, desperate for entry into a world of comforting stability in the style of Evelina and Camilla. Like Cecilia, she is deprived of her rightful inheritance, but she is also concerned much more crudely with the mechanics of sheer survival. In the grim critique of English mores which follows, Burney has lost interest in satirising particular moral failings or in laughing at the sophistication and extravagance of a frivolous community, as she did in *Cecilia* and *Camilla*. Instead, she mounts a vicious attack on the pettiness, cruelty, complacency and fundamental intolerance of which that community is composed. No wonder reviewers found the book disconcerting, for the focus of attack had been diverted and a more comprehensive view of English life is the result.

Burney fully understood the reason for the hostile critical reception. 'I attribute it to the false expectation universally spread that the Book was to be a picture of France', she commented ruefully. Juliet's exclusion from any definable social role makes her into a classic outcast and as she wanders through the country in search of employment and a home, she is given opportunity to observe and analyse different life styles and to discover the numerous dangers that both urban and rural life conceal.

Still the apologia suggests Burney's divided loyalties. At the same time that she makes a point of affirming her neutrality she is forced to admit that writing a novel about contemporary life, by its very nature, must be a political act. Like other writers of her generation, Fanny Burney was keenly alive to the fact that no sensitive observer of social change could afford to ignore large-scale movements and shifts in thought. She had lived through one of the most explosive periods of European history and her closeness to the experience of both French and English families gave her a unique position as qualified commentator on the crisis that had penetrated deep into the consciousness of both nations. An acute understanding of the impact of history pervades *The Wanderer* and is in part responsible for its tone of formality and alienation. Burney was after all writing in the middle of a war and her own situation with her Anglo-French sympathies was dangerously fragile. 'To attempt to delineate, in whatever form, any picture of actual human life, without reference to the French Revolution', she wrote sharply, 'would be as little possible as to give an idea of the English government without reference to our own: for not more unavoidably is the last blended with the history of our nation than the first with every intellectual survey of the present times'. For the first time Burney brought the interpretative approach to current affairs that permeates her journal to bear on her fictional material but the result is unfortunately not the artistic success we might have

expected. For in wanting to describe the devastating effects
of recent events, Fanny Burney was torn between her wish to
appear dutiful to the country of her birth and her political
conscience. Careful to demonstrate a proper sense of
patriotic feeling, she was also keen to be an accurate, and as
she thought, objective recorder and to introduce her own
privileged viewpoint into the hotly debated matters of the
past decade. Of course Burney remained a loyal English
subject but her years in Paris had distanced her from British
culture. The Napoleonic wars had created a fierce anti-
French feeling and Burney's refusal to endorse wholeheartedly the passionate jingoism of her countrymen was
bound to be unpopular.

To avoid being accused of partisanship, she set her novel in
the midst of the Reign of Terror, hoping, somewhat naively,
that the retrospective framework would testify to the
impartiality of her 'observations'. So her story opens in the
regime of Robespierre: a boatful of English refugees are
escaping from the turmoil of Revolutionary France to the
safety of their homeland. For Burney's heroine, however,
that safety is illusory and an implicit parallel is drawn
between the two countries. The theme of exile, personally
meaningful to both the D'Arblays themselves, here is
invested with symbolic value in the study of Juliet's rejection
by the society in which she seeks refuge.

Not surprisingly, Burney found herself the butt of
sardonic reviewers, who, despite her disclaimers and her
scrupulous avoidance of the dreaded word 'Bonaparte',
suspected her of enemy sympathies and found her guilty of
treachery in what they termed her 'little annotatory flatteries
of the scourge of the human race'.[2]

Residence in France had given Mme D'Arblay confidence
and authority. Her personal sense of literary decorum was
still, however, plagued by the precedents of her youth and
much of *The Wanderer* tellingly reveals the fact that it had
been written fifteen years earlier. 1814, the year *The*

Wanderer was published, also saw the appearance of *Mansfield Park* and *Waverley*, novels immensely assured in their handling of fictional techniques, subtly balancing personal and public issues against the larger processes of historical change. With Austen and Scott the novel had truly come of age and both Burney's defence of the form for its didactic value and her awkward plot and repetitive episodic structure seemed to belong to a past era. Technically, *The Wanderer* is a failure but it is pervaded with a consciousness of social injustice that marks it as very much of its time and in its response to the concern with feminist ideas that had been engendered by post Revolutionary radical activists it also counts as something of a milestone in the history of women's writing.

The complicated background to the main action of the novel is not revealed to the reader until Volume IV. Juliet Granville, the offspring of a secret marriage between an English lord and a lowly but beautiful paragon, has been brought up in France after her mother's death and her father's remarriage. During the Revolution, she is forced into a form of marriage with a commissary of Robespierre's, greedy for the dowry of £6000 which her father's family have offered as a bribe to any French suitor. Her father dead, Juliet agrees to the wedding in order to save her guardian, a French bishop, from the guillotine. She manages to escape to England immediately after the ceremony but dare not declare her true identity until she has been assured of the bishop's safety. A series of coincidences makes her firstly an intimate in the family circle of the Granvilles, where she remains incognito, while forming loving relationships with her half-brother and sister, and secondly brings her face to face with her maternal uncle, who has full documentary evidence to allow her to claim her rightful inheritance, far exceeding the £6000 dowry. At the end of the novel her marriage is annulled, her French citizen husband conveniently dies anyway, her name is revealed and her faithful English suitor,

Albert Harleigh, claims her hand. The movement from
danger and anonymity to security and identity that was
begun with Burney's first novel, *Evelina*, has now come full
circle. The extravagant denouement serves, however, merely
to frame the central matter of the novel, which concerns
Juliet's experiences in England, when, unknown and
penniless, she struggles to make her own way in the world.

The courtesy books of the 1790s had concentrated on the
very real problems of conduct faced by girls fresh from the
schoolroom when they came to tread a path through the
delicate hazards and myriad confusions of the adult social
scene. Their tone of cautiousness was in part a reflection of
the general indeterminacies in thinking about women's roles.
Twenty years later, in a climate where Inchbald, Edgeworth
and Austen had been acclaimed and where literate women
were taken for granted, female novelists were more certain of
their ground. Misgivings about masculine categorisation of
women had emerged in educational tracts, political
pamphlets and in more suggestive fictional undercurrents
and in the context of a rapidly expanding market for women,
both as readers and writers, female problems assumed a
dimension that invited a wholescale reassessment of their
treatment. As attitudes crystallised, woman alone became
the central subject of most female fictions. Novels as
different as Ann Radcliffe's *The Mysteries of Udolpho* (1792),
Mary Wollstonecraft's *Maria* (1797), Mary Brunton's *Self
Control* (1812) and Jane Austen's *Mansfield Park* (1814) all
dealt with the ability of their heroines to combat a hostile
environment. Romantic or realist in their approach, women
had at last grasped the fact that the myth of virtue rewarded
was largely a male imposition and their novels are permeated
by images of doubt, anger, fear and distress. Motifs of
confinement, abandonment and discrimination abound.
Young women are required to face situations which call on all
their resources of courage and endurance and, whether the
setting is Gothic or domestic, the novels share a common

assumption: that women's lives are often composed of suffering, inflicted on them by an unfair system, and their chances of self-realisation are heavily compromised. Fanny Burney had always understood that this was an issue to be taken seriously and in *The Wanderer* she creates a dramatic fable of women's experience through the extremist and emphatic study of her heroine's isolation.

Juliet Granville enters the story heavily disguised, her skin darkened, her face apparently scarred and wearing ragged clothes. Her journey across the Channel, in a boat filled with English passengers, is an accurate indication of the reception she can expect to find when she lands. Antagonistic or indifferent, the passengers are largely impervious to her discomforts, and Juliet emerges as a representative of her sex. Without a name, her true appearance concealed, her gender is her only identifying characteristic. Her portrayal focuses more sharply than ever before in Burney's fiction the question of what it means to be a woman in early nineteenth-century England. How does she acquire identity? How can she be classified? Juliet eludes easy categorisation and the social prejudices that greet her on her arrival and throughout her vicissitudes are not just class barriers but gender traps as well. Because she is an unknown quantity, those people whom Juliet encounters reveal their own confusions in not knowing how to treat her. Social response, Burney suggests, is determined according to a series of signs and Juliet continually puts out misleading signals that create a false impression of her status. Her original face, patched and stained, betokens a lowly rank: it hides both her beauty and her refinement. She is assumed to be a servant and spoken to accordingly. Washed and dressed differently, her physical charms become apparent but still her name is withheld, her purse is lost and she has no friends prepared to come forward and protect her. The mystery both intrigues and repels her associates, whose reactions vary according to their own sense of charity but who all illuminate the codification of the nature of social acceptance. An unpleasant form of self-knowledge is thus forced on Juliet. 'What is woman unprotected?' she asks bitterly. 'She is pronounced on only from outward semblance:– and indeed what other criterion has the world? Can it read the heart?' For it is as a woman that her disadvantages multiply and Burney presents bluntly the special nature of the problems which face a woman entirely alone, when self-reliance is an inadequate insurance against starvation.

For Juliet's trials, symbolic though they are, also demonstrate the very practical difficulties of survival. The basic necessities of food, money and shelter are pressing realities in the uncaring world that Juliet inhabits. Her attempts to earn her own living, a new departure for a middle-class fictional heroine but an experience only too familiar to Burney herself, add to the complexities of her portrayal. As a lady, Juliet is ill-equipped to fend for herself when the traditional means of provision are removed. She tries first to utilise her 'accomplishments' by giving music lessons, and then by fine needlework. When these fail, she gains employment in a milliner's shop and later in a mantua maker's workroom, each step more degrading than the last. Ironically, her most humiliating occupation is that which smacks most of respectability, as paid companion to an elderly widow, the tyrannical Mrs Ireton, who, in denying Juliet's right to be treated as an individual, brings to a climax the images of exploitation that have been busily collecting. Juliet's displacement in this household interestingly anticipates the fears of Austen's Jane Fairfax about the 'governess trade', as well as the more sustained pictures of isolation and indignity found in the Brontës' descriptions of this type of genteel servitude.

Not only Juliet's insufficiency but the vulnerability of working women everywhere is exposed in this novel. At one point, Juliet's friend, Gabriella, tries to run a haberdashery shop but her ingrained honesty, part and parcel of her code of

undeviating female virtue, is a severe liability in the
mercantile life. A woman of high ethical standards cannot
survive in a competitive trade where 'unpractised in every
species of business, she has no criterion whence to calculate
its chances, or be aware of its changes'. Life is a gamble for
women on their own and financial security is what
determines the luxury of moral freedom. 'I lost my purse',
comments Juliet, 'and away with it flew my fancied
independence, my ability to live as I pleased.' The millinery
assistants, dependent for their livelihood on their ability to
please others, are abused by their employer and patronised
by the customers. What is worse, they become the unofficial
goods on display for male perusal. Burney plots in some
detail a seduction attempt on one gullible sixteen-year-old
seamstress, who, innocent and romantic, would fall willing
victim to the snares of a practised rake. Sexuality is a danger
that menaces all women and men are perceived as a constant
threat.

Matters are no different in the countryside. On a farm in
the New Forest, Juliet sees the fathers and sons assume
preferential treatment as their right, the boys 'domineering
over their sisters and mocking their mother'. The pastoral
ideal is quickly demolished in Burney's acerbic view of rural
life, where a farmer's wife exists as little more than a slave to
the brutal whims of her despotic husband. Female labourers
toil without relief and have the added torment of sexual
harassment from casual predatory workmen. Juliet, after a
timely rescue from three potential rapists, having sought
shelter in a wood, is fully awakened to such debasement. 'Is it
only under the domestic roof', she asks despairingly, '– that
roof to me denied – that woman can know safety, respect and
honour?'

The real adventurousness of this sort of subject matter is
somewhat diminished by the handling of the character of
Juliet herself, for the features that Burney provides to
distinguish her heroine as a woman of sensitivity and breeding

conform to the conventional model of feminine decorousness
as specified by Dr Gregory and his ilk. Juliet is revealed early
on as beautiful and graceful, with a commendable sense of
modesty and a well-modulated speaking voicce. When it
comes to demonstrating her advanced level of education,
however, Burney can produce little evidence other than her
elegant handwriting. It is at this stage that Juliet most
conspicuously takes on the status of a romance figure. She is a
fairy-tale heroine referred to more than once in the text as a
'princess in disguise'. Her exceptional beauty and charm are
accompanied with other appropriate talents: outstanding
musical, drawing and dramatic ability and a prodigious
memory which enables her to learn a complicated theatrical
role in a matter of hours. What Burney illustrates is the
disparity between the permitted parameters of middle-class
femininity and any attempt at genuine self-sufficiency. The
principles of propriety are diametrically opposed to
independent existence. The position is encapsulated in
Harleigh's plea to Juliet to refrain from taking part in a public
concert, although she is desperate for money and needs to
advertise her talents to get pupils, because it would mean
'deviating . . . from the long-beaten track of female
timidity.'

For Juliet this is catch-22. To submit to the approved
pattern precipitates degradation and penury. She cannot
accept cash presents from men, although besieged with
offers, because of the sexual implications. Her lack of choice
is reiterated throughout the novel in a series of images of
pursuit and imprisonment. We see her being chased around a
garden trying to avoid capture, being caged in a summer
house, locked in a chamber with the key tantalisingly
withheld and even on one occasion ingeniously pinned to the
ground by an old man's crutches. This presentation of female
subjection elicited some curious responses. 'A Novelist can
claim no necessity for describing a young and accomplished
female as remaining in the house of a woman who had treated

her with such brutal insult', one reviewer complained angrily. 'Such a lesson should not have been presented to the large portion of the female community in whose society *The Wanderer* is destined to circulate.'[3] He seems rather to have missed Burney's point.

But Burney develops the complexities of women's dilemma in a fascinating, if perhaps over-schematic, contrast between Juliet and a more militant feminist figure, Elinor Joddrel. These two represent opposing policies in women's struggle for an independent life and they turn the novel into a vivid and dramatic debate about strategy. By 1814, Mary Wollstonecraft had been dead for seventeen years but the aftermath of her *A Vindication of the Rights of Women* was still powerfully felt. The *Vindication* had been published in 1792. It was a brilliant piece of polemical writing, springing from a deeply felt concern about women's education and yet written almost by accident and thrown together in a brief six weeks. High-minded, passionate and rhetorical, it was clearly the product of a vigorous if rather unruly intellect and it stridently concentrated many of the ideas about women's roles which had been more tentatively floated by others. Wollstonecraft had undertaken a massive task. Her book, burning with indignation about sexual injustice, contained a disturbing combination of historical, political and philosophical propaganda. Wollstonecraft compared the situation of women with slavery, a condition which she saw perpetuated by a male-dominated social system. Women, she argued persuasively, had been conditioned into adopting an artificially passive role, cheated of their natural rights and insultingly patronised by men who 'advise us only to render ourselves gentle, domestic brutes!' She demanded wholesale changes in education to allow girls to grow up and develop their individual talents on a par with boys and later to be given the opportunity to train for a career and establish independent lives. Her denial of any fundamental gender difference lay at the heart of her thesis. 'I do earnestly wish', she asserted, 'to see the distinction of sex confounded in society, unless where love animates the behaviour. For this distinction is, I am firmly persuaded, the foundation of the weakness of character ascribed to women; is the cause why the understanding is neglected, whilst accomplishments are acquired with sedulous care.'[4] Wollstonecraft's insights into the inadequacies of women's current situation are not dissimilar to Burney's but in her approach to dealing with the subject of 'female difficulties', she is the absolute antithesis.

Fully recognising its limits, Burney had come to terms with the protective folds of tradition and she perceived the threat to order and security implied in active female militancy. Certainly in *The Wanderer*, Elinor's directness does not achieve the positive results she hopes for and her fate embodies Burney's mistrust of outspokenness as set against the more reliable, if more insidious, survival techniques adopted by Juliet. For these two characters, united in their common understanding of female oppression, are conceived as opposites in terms of the tactics they employ and together they form an ironic enquiry into the acceptable face of feminism. Always attracted by the idea of female defiance, Burney had previously relegated her aggressive women to the sidelines but in this novel she makes Elinor's stance a focal point of interest. She also makes her young and pretty, unlike the earlier, more mature figures of Mesdames Selwyn, Delvile and Arlbery.

Elinor cannot be laughed off or ignored. She is voluble, forceful and stimulating. Intelligent and energetic, she is, like Wollstonecraft, an enthusiastic convert to the ideals of the French Revolution, although inattentive to their more destructive effects. Her devotion to the cause of emancipation enables Burney to provide her with some dynamic criticism of the patriarchal system, criticism that is never repudiated in the text. 'Men . . . would keep us from every office but making puddings and pies for their own precious palates', Elinor derisively tells Juliet. 'Oh woman!

poor subdued woman! thou art as dependent mentally upon the arbitrary customs of man, as man is, corporeally, upon the established laws of his country.' Elinor is a formidable champion of women's liberation. Spirited and eloquent, her speeches penetrate to the heart of the anomalous situation in which Juliet finds herself, trapped by the masculine double standard. For, as Elinor so shrewdly infers about men,

'This woman, whom they estimate thus below, they elevate above themselves. They require from her, in defiance of their examples – in defiance of their lures! – angelical perfection. She must be mistress of her passions; she must never listen to her inclinations; she must not take a step of which the purport is not visible; she must not pursue a measure of which she cannot publish the motive; she must always be guided by reason, though they deny her understanding!'

The implications of Juliet's experiences stand as sufficient testimony to the validity of Elinor's views but Burney categorically refuses to accept the revolutionary tendencies which she portrays as accompanying these attitudes. Although she might be in sympathy with many of Elinor's theories, Burney places them in a context of practical realities that constantly demonstrate the inexpedience of radical change. For, in her challenge to the conventions, Elinor's undoubted enterprise does her no good at all. Scorning reticence, she defies custom and takes the initiative in declaring her love for Harleigh, the best in the way of a hero there is. When he rejects her proposals, she becomes hysterical and tries to commit suicide – twice. 'Without someone to love, this world is a desert',[5] Mary Wollstonecraft had once confessed, and despite Elinor's insistence on logic she is shown as subject to uncontrolled emotionalism and as dependent on masculine approval as her meeker sisters.

In her blind attachment to abstract idealism and her wild actions, Elinor may well have been modelled on the 'hyena in petticoats' herself. Indeed Godwin's account of his wife, *Memoirs of the Author of a Vindication of the Rights of Women*, which appeared in 1798, after her death, unfortunately did nothing to endear Wollstonecraft's views to a more conservative feminist audience. By laying bare the unconventional details of her life as a haphazard succession of mishaps, veering between extremes of fervour and desolation, Godwin made Mary's fairly moderate relationships with men seem outrageous and her reputation acquired a notoriety which terrified more wary reformers. Female militancy and sexual irregularity became irrevocably linked in the public mind. The incongruity between Wollstonecraft's emphasis on rationalism and her own impulsive and erratic experience could hardly have escaped notice as astute as Burney's and may well have influenced the association of radicalism with verbal fluency and rash judgement that we find in the conception of Elinor.

'What a terrible perversion is here of intellect!' comments Harleigh on Elinor. 'What a confusion of ideas! what an inextricable chaos of false principles, exaggerated feelings and imaginary advancement in new doctrines of life!' Wollstonecraft's atheism, dwelt on in the *Memoirs*, is repeated as part of Elinor's all embracing adoption of rebellious postures, which, in removing the restraints of orthodoxy, simultaneously invites despair. True to the fabular structure of the narrative, Harleigh, loved by both women, chooses the one who most closely conforms to the norm of male desires, the demure and silent Juliet. For Elinor, the fight for independence is presented as a game; for Juliet, it consists of immediate arduous tasks to be tackled. Elinor's attempted suicide, reminiscent of Mary Wollstonecraft's attempts after she was discarded by Gilbert Imlay, her lover, are interpreted as attention-seeking devices by one whose liberal opinions are a luxury that women such as Juliet cannot afford. For Burney's heroine, the concept of life and death are meaningful constituents of her daily uphill struggle for existence.

In fact, a curious role reversal takes place in the course of the novel, as the narrative form offers the paradoxical view that sensibility is in itself a rational course of action. Elinor's vehemence and volubility is discredited as uncontrolled. Juliet, who is modelled on the pattern of conventional sensibility, generous, demonstrative, affectionate and responsive, yet understands at bottom that 'all chance of security hung upon the exertion of good sense, and the right use of reason.' Burney does not dismiss the female mind. Indeed, she is scathing about men in the novel who criticise the French for choosing a woman to personify the goddess of Reason. Rather, Juliet's feminine pose of delicacy and restraint belies her inner courage and is in itself something of a decoy. The mask she wears at the beginning of the novel is more than just a narrative ploy but reflects the indispensability of disguise for women as a means of protection. Elinor's emotional honesty and her directness lead her to disaster, as Burney demonstrates that artifice is the only sure method of female survival.

Fanny Burney goes further in her analysis of the intricacies of socio-sexual relations. For it is the female community which constitutes the basic power structure of this novel. Women's lives are lived in a largely female world and women, while taking their lead from the dominant patriarchal culture, are responsible for controlling the fortunes of their own sex. None of the male characters in this book really assumes anything approaching a human personality. Men are one-dimensional ciphers – the courtly hero, the libertine, the callow youth, the bluff sailor – lifted from tired literary conventions. It is the women who are invested with substance and women who have authority over women. Mothers must approve of Juliet, if their daughters are to be her pupils; dowagers hold the key to poverty or subsistence.

When there are suspicions voiced about the Wanderer's origins, she is immediately ostracised, and once female patronage has been withdrawn, she is abandoned to the mercy of male profligacy, antipathetic to women's interests.

It is women's notice that determines Juliet's fate and the real enemies she has to grapple with are women, entrenched in positions of solidarity. Here, Burney was almost certainly drawing on her own experiences of humiliation at the hands of dictatorial older women. Her stepmother, and her sister, Mrs Young, had made the young Burney girls and their cousins suffer miserably throughout their adolescence. More recently, the bullying Mrs Schwellenberg in the Royal household had interfered intolerably with Fanny's privacy, and had forced on her countless niggling privations. In *The Wanderer*, the 'three Furies', Mrs Maple, Mrs Ireton and Mrs Howel, are domineering middle-aged women who make Juliet's life a nightmare, with their trivial persecutions and displays of authoritarianism which do their best to undermine her hold on self. Indebted to men for their status, these widows hang on to it grimly, riding roughshod over those who fail to conform to the outward standards of rank and wealth that dictate their narrow version of acceptability.

To offset this, Burney places a parallel value on female friendship. This was a subject of permanent interest in women's fiction of the period, satirised in its excesses by Jane Austen, who yet recognised its worth. Burney's novels reflect a deepening concern with the significance of the rapport between women. Evelina's relationship with Miss Mirvan is overtaken by the greater emphasis given to Cecilia's expectations of her friends and her joy in discovering a soul mate in Mrs Delvile. The importance of sisterly affection and the correct choice of a friend becomes a central theme in the more moralistic climate of *Camilla*. Female friendship overcomes considerations of age and rank in favour of gender sympathy and, in *The Wanderer*, it provides a lifeline for a woman alone. Lady Aurora Granville, Selina, Elinor and

Gabriella are all perceived as possible vital sources of emotional comfort, practical support and outlets for Juliet's self-expression. The confidante is seen as an essential element in a world where public articulacy for women is condemned and the sharing of the experience of deprivation is an important basis for understanding between members of the same sex.

Like the secret that Juliet carries, Fanny Burney's novels are deceptive in their forms. They appear to become increasingly reactionary in the world view that they offer, diminishing the importance of the individual perspective, crushing any sign of divergence from the conventional norm and attaching greater and greater weight to the objective moral and political ideology and external social reality. Characters are allowed less and less licence. Their self-expression is curbed and signs of originality are sharply criticised. Evelina was allowed to keep her private opinions intact but Elinor is devastated and Juliet a cardboard cutout. Such a tempting reading is, however, misleading and we should be wary of dismissing Burney's conservatism as totally obstructionist. For what we find as the novels progress is in fact a greater reliance on subterfuge, both in form and content, as the sympathies of the texts suggest an uneasy radicalism. Elinor's behaviour may be outwardly condemned but the force of her arguments is justified by much of the novel's action. The attempt to smash the mould of male imposed patterns, both in practical and literary terms, is, Burney suggests, a futile one if conducted in public. It is only in the world of private experience that women can construct their own definitive identities. They must work as undercover agents to dismantle the fiction of male superiority and to replace it with an alternative is a slow and delicate process. Emotion and common sense coexist in the creation of a female persona in the sour, realistic assessment of *The Wanderer*, as Juliet and Elinor form two sides of the feminist coin.

Necessarily distancing herself from the immediate and the spontaneous to conform to literary conventions, Burney, in her final fictional effort, proves how inadequate for her are public forms of expression. For her most honest statements of self, we must turn to the literary exercise which illuminated and accompanied so much of her professional career, her personal journals.

7 Journals and Plays

'But perhaps I keep no journal', ventures Catherine Morland to Henry Tilney early on in Jane Austen's *Northanger Abbey*. His reply is one of sardonic incredulity.

'Perhaps you are not sitting here in this room, and I am not sitting by you. These are points in which a doubt is equally permissible. Not keep a journal! How are your absent cousins to understand the tenour of your life in Bath without one? How are the civilities and compliments of every day to be related as they ought to be remembered, and the particular state of your complexion and curl of your hair to be described in all their diversities, without having constant recourse to a journal? – My dear madam, I am not so ignorant of young ladies' ways as you wish to believe me; . . . .[1]

Poor Catherine, naively visualising herself a heroine, while lacking the proper literary accoutrements! But behind the wry humour of Austen's remarks lies a shrewd résumé of the real significance of journal keeping in female lives of this period. Often isolated from family and childhood friends by marriage or by journeys such as Catherine's, women were able to use journals both as a means of establishing communication with others and as a private record of their own experiences, a creation of self in the writing and an affirmation of self in the reading of the entries. In the prevailing climate of incertitude about women's nature and function, journals validated identity. They provided a permitted outlet for self-expression, a welcome relief to imaginative and articulate young ladies, trained to a career of public silence. By the end of the eighteenth century, as Jane Austen nicely suggests, journal keeping had become a necessary and almost commonplace activity for many middle-class, literate women.

The journals and letters of Fanny Burney constitute one of the outstanding documents of the century. Combining the artless freedom of direct personal address with the literary control of the conscious stylist, they illuminate the dichotomy between the private and public selves that contributes so tellingly to the ambiguity of her published writings. They provide too a unique perspective on the processes of history, for Burney's life spanned an age of social and political upheaval. Coming from a highly cultivated household, she was pushed involuntarily into the inner circles of contemporary literati and from there into an intimate if unwilling relationship with the Royal family at Windsor and at Kew. She lived through a period of major disturbances. The Gordon riots, the French Revolution and Waterloo were all events which had an immediate bearing on her life. Her journals, while recognising the far-reaching implications of such turmoil, dramatise convincingly the centrality of its effect on the individual experience. The diaries in fact demonstrate how the rhythms of one woman's life can be integrated into and fortified against the wider, more diffuse social world that threatens to overwhelm them. History is mediated through the single consciousness and it is the nature of the individual response which emerges triumphant as the truth that we relate to. It is only when Fanny Burney, glancing through the window of her Paris apartment, sees her husband mounted in full war regalia ready to ride away, that the full horror of their situation hits her. The magnitude of war impinges on the perception via the casual detail and the world of private feeling is what defines the impact of the world of public affairs.

As well as the diary entries and lengthy autobiographical accounts, often written some years after the events themselves took place, approximately two thousand of Fanny Burney's private letters have survived intact. For over seventy years, she wrote virtually every day, sometimes sending up to five daily letters if circumstances so demanded. The value of these writings to Burney herself was immeasurable. In 1815, forced to flee hurriedly from war-torn Paris, her deepest regret was that in her panic, she had left behind 'All my MSS! – My beloved Father's! my family papers! – my letters of all my life! my Susan's Journals!!' The precious manuscripts were prized beyond clothes, furniture or other material possessions. Far more than mere documentation, they had become Burney's roots, invested with a significance that incorporated her past, her relationships and her very identity. They were the palpable evidence that her life had shape and meaning.

She had begun her first diary in March 1768, in fine adolescent style. 'To whom dare I reveal my private opinion of my nearest relations?', she wrote half jokingly but nevertheless testing out and defining her own requirements. 'My secret thoughts of my dearest friends? My own hopes, fears, reflections and dislikes? – Nobody! To Nobody then will I write my Journal. . . .' From the beginning concealment was vital and disclosure a fear not to be contemplated. However innocently, the journal allowed a sense of liberty to the thoughts which, because they were her own, were too seditious to be spoken aloud. Secrecy was the necessary ballast for her social reticence and she was soon warned against journal keeping as 'the most dangerous employment young persons can have – that it makes them record things which ought *not* to be recorded, but instantly forgot'. But the joy she found in the act of writing overcame any more cautious scruples as her mental freedom discovered

itself behind the barriers of domestic restriction. More than
this, memories were to be fixed and could act as a delicate
measuring stick of her personal growth. 'I cannot express the
pleasure I have in writing down my thoughts at the very
moment', she confided to the tight-lipped Miss Nobody, '–
my opinion of people when I first see them, and how I alter,
or how confirm myself in it.'

Her first letters to this imaginary confidante – for her
correspondents of later years were at that time still living at
home with her – helped Burney to counter the intrusive
reality of the world around her. She needed to contain and to
rearticulate experience in order to derive its meaning and
people and events lost some of their awesomeness when
reduced to manageable size by her pen.

Fanny Burney's journals openly confront the problem
central to all artists of how to select and make sense of the
inchoate mass of experience with which one is constantly
faced. Burney's need for structure was satisfied by the
exercise of consciously organising her thoughts. After M.
D'Arblay's departure for battle, paralysed by the shock of
parting after that meaningful glance through the window,
she realised that she 'could execute nothing corporeally, for I
could arrange nothing intellectually. My ideas were
bewildered; my senses seemed benumbed; my mind was a
chaos'. Mental order was a prerequisite of Burney's life and
her journals became her means of clarifying past experience
and regulating her procedures for future action. The early
diary, which became dominated by her long letters to Mr
Crisp, was infused with the same ebullient spirit of laughter
that dominates *Evelina* as Burney reduced disarray to
recognisable signs and framed her encounters and
acquaintances in comic portraiture. Folly enchanted her.
'She is the verriest *booby* I ever knew', she reported
delightedly on a fellow guest at a house party, launching into
such a long and jubilant description of poor Miss W's
stupidity that she was eventually quite sorry to leave her, 'for

I had by no means the entertainment after she was gone; indeed I told her that I was sure we should not be *so merry* when she was gone – and she seemed extremely pleased at the compliment'.

But Fanny Burney's diary was more than a training ground for her art as caricaturist. It served a variety of purposes for her and its place in her daily routine was complex and subtle. Above all, her diary attests to the primacy of solitude and the need to clutch at her threatened identity. Although she never lost her eye for the ridiculous as she grew older, her later entries were to become increasingly sombre in tone, echoing her growing awareness of alienation. Deluged with the notoriety brought by her first two novels, Fanny Burney turned to her diary as a refuge, a shield for her personality from the prying eyes of strangers. In 1785, when she was first introduced to life at Court, she was able to mock the royal obsession with ceremony and could parody the stilted regime in a letter to her sister Hetty containing *Directions for coughing, sneezing or moving before the King and Queen*. But as the pettiness of court life swamped her the officiousness ground down her spontaneous light-heartedness. The private writings were then a lifeline. 'If to you alone I show myself in these dark colours', she wrote pitifully from Windsor to her beloved sister, Susan, 'can you blame the plan I have intentionally been forming – namely to wean myself from myself – to lessen all my affections – to curb all my wishes – to deaden all my sensations?' The privations imposed upon her could be endured only if she negated all natural impulse in carrying out her daily rituals. In her emotional isolation, her journal was her sole salvation, affirming the existence of a world which responded still to her humanity.

Through the medium of the journal, she forged her links with her family, consolidating her own sense of self through those fundamental relationships which allowed for total honesty. Throughout her life, distanced from those dearest

to her, by the vicissitudes of fortune, she relied on the
writings for consolation. They became a vehicle for
tenderness, capable of an intimacy which was otherwise
beyond her reach. 'Read at your leisure, rien de presse – c'est
pour vous endormir la nuit', reads a typical heading on a
letter to her husband. And 'Why – why – Oh Alexander! this
cruel silence?', she implores her renegade son, an atypical
Burney in his reluctance to put pen to paper. Burney's fiction
always concerned itself centrally with isolation. Her heroines
are alone, facing a frightening environment, fraught with the
menace of the unknown. Their retreat is in the security of the
family and their most perilous moments occur when this
umbrella of comfort is withdrawn. Personal relationships
protect them from the inquisitive society which threatens
their precarious sense of their own identity. In the journals,
the key to the enigma of Burney's career, we find this pattern
repeated emphatically. Private experience is enduring and
real, distinct from social artificiality. 'Such a set of tittle
tattle, prittle prattle visitants!' Fanny Burney wrote
disgustedly to Mr Crisp. 'I am so sick of the ceremony and
fuss of these fall lall people! So much dressing – chit chat –
complimentary nonsense – In short – a Country Town is my
detestation –'. For Burney it is the family which stands firm
as the rock on which the individual can depend, is succoured
and indeed is formed and which provides an utterly
trustworthy source of support and self-realisation. 'Your 7th
letter is just arrived – my beloved friend', runs one thankful
letter to her husband,' – & I shall pass a day of genial revival.
Their effect upon me in every sort of way is nearly wonderful
to myself! Oh remember a single *Bonjour, dated*, when you
are pressed for time, will at least keep me from such fits of
morne mélancolie as undermine secretly & slowly, but surely,
the poor harassed machine, of which the inside outworks the
outside . . . and to write to you, when I think you have time
to read me excites my *second* best sensations. The *First* best –
need I name?'

Fanny Burney was fully alive to the therapeutic effects of her personal writing. Awaiting news of Waterloo, she comforted herself with her journal. 'Lowered, disappointed, disheartened, I returned to my pen, with which alone I was able in pouring forth my fears to attract back my hopes & in recording my miseries, to imbibe instinctively the sympathy which had the power, magnetic to sooth them.' The journal was a means of coming to terms with and exorcising her own anxieties. Sure of her audience, she could write freely, unhampered by having to live up to the anticipations of a clamorous and critical public. The journals both protected and liberated her personality and provide a startling insight into the mechanisms of her creativity.

Recollection, for Fanny Burney, was a creative act and in the privacy of her diary and correspondence she was at her most potent as a literary artist. Constantly we find her reworking material in order to produce the maximum narrative effect. Fashioning her experience into its most telling form, meticulous observation combines with artistic sensitivity. With no expectations or standards to live up to, other than her own, her work succeeds superbly, springing from the drama of direct personal involvement. We find stunning accounts of extraordinary experiences. Her description of her operation for breast cancer undertaken without anaesthetic in 1811 is economical, spare and chilling in its lack of sentimentality. It is a powerful testament of physical and psychological courage as well as a masterpiece of narrative organisation. Horror and desolation combine too in her eye witness account of the aftermath of Waterloo.

For more than a week from this time I never approached my Window but to witness sights of wretchedness. Maimed, wounded, bleeding, mutilated, tortured victims of this exterminating contest, passed by every minute; the fainting, the sick, the dying & the Dead, on brancards, in

Carts, in Wagons, succeeded one another without intermission. . . .

In this, as in the other sustained analyses of emotionally charged experiences, the effect is produced by the interpretative mind, seeking out significance through literary organisation.

The most absorbing of these lengthy autobiographical entries were all written with several years hindsight. A conscious artist, Burney imposed order on the raw material of circumstance, given the distance and leisure of retrospection. Frequently she emerges as the heroine of her own story. *The Ilfracombe Journal* depicts Fanny trapped in a cave by the incoming tide, when out walking one sunny afternoon looking for pebbles on the Devon beach. With her pet dog as her sole companion, she discovers too late that the water levels have cut off her exit and, as the weather changes, she despairs of escape. It is a tale of adventure, highlighting the elements of danger and suspense through her progressive perceptions of her plight. Her eventual rescuer, however, was later to pooh-pooh the affair. 'The lady's adventure was greatly exaggerated', he disparagingly commented. '– She was in no real danger – The sea had not come up to her. She was not clinging to the rock – She was seated on the sand –'. Is memory so fallible? Clearly, for Burney, the imagination defines the nature of our experience and it is always subjective truth with which she is concerned.

One of the most deeply moving sections of the journals is that which plots the stages of M. D'Arblay's final illness from rectal cancer. The narrative is as much a presentation of the process of bereavement as it is of dying. Coming to terms with the reality of death, both for the patient and the survivor was a process of slow and painful knowledge, acquired more reluctantly and bitterly by Fanny than by her husband. Writing about it two years afterwards, she had by no means recovered. 'I will give this expansion to my feelings for a few minutes – a poor half hour – every evening I pass alone, to unburthen the loaded heart from the weight of suppression during the long and heavy day.' By reliving the agony of suffering, she hoped to alleviate the tortured memory. In scrupulous detail, she described the fluctuation of her own feelings, her sensitivity to each of his spasms of pain and the long, grim process of decline, from the time when D'Arblay struggled to conceal his symptoms, so as to stand to greet Queen Charlotte on her visit to Bath, to his fading away of the last fortnight and the death itself. The coherent style, restrained and often lyrical, is in sharp contrast to the hasty, broken note of two years earlier scribbled when she was overcome by the immediacy of grief to her sister Charlotte. 'Oh my Charlotte', begins the attempt at communication '– – – my dear – – dear Charlotte – – how can I write and not break your heart – – I have stopt my Pen – I have checked – laid by – but 'tis vainly I strive to write what would not afflict you. . . .' Mental composure was impossible and silence the only solution. Her return to writing was analagous to a return to life.

In *The Wanderer*, Fanny Burney showed her contempt for suicide. She held an indefatigable belief in survival and her journals constantly testify to her will to challenge the odds weighted against her. As a child, her mother's death had penetrated deep into her consciousness. She refused to be comforted, as if acknowledging her need for private grief. As a young woman, at Court, she confronted innumerable hardships – extreme cold, late hours, exhaustion, nervous tension and emotional deprivation. Her married happiness was short-lived and interrupted by frequent separations. The exigencies of war, economic worries and serious family anxieties all took their toll. In her fifties, alone in a foreign country, she braved the terrors of surgery and fought for life in an age when patients were frequently known to die from operative shock as much as from disease. But despite her reputation for fragility, Fanny survived her sisters, brothers, her husband and her son, together with generations of younger Burneys who should, according to the laws of nature, have outlived her. Her resilience was formidable. 'There is something in this freedom of repining that I could by no means approve', she commented severely after a depressing conversation with a particularly misanthropic young lady as early as 1780. 'I could not think it consistent with either truth or religion to cherish such notions'. However miserable her circumstances, Fanny Burney never gave way to the temptations of despair. As her novels describe female difficulties, so her diary records her personal fortitude in an unstable and often inimical environment. Her journals were the therapy which restored her faith in the solidity of her own history and identity by containing and controlling the shifting experience which confronted her.

Fanny Burney's novels show her public face: they make their appeal to order and system and show young women's progress from exclusion to conformity. No allowance can be made for the deviant or the renegade in Burney's uncompromising regimen of female survival. Yet, her fiction often contains characters and episodes which invite sharp criticism of the culture she professes to endorse. As in Burney's life, the private thoughts could be said to be at variance with, but a necessary corollary to, her public persona of unquestioning acceptance. The ambivalence which is such a striking feature of her writing is illuminated further by a reading of her little-known plays, especially the four comedies, *The Witlings* (1779), *Love and Fashion* (1799), *A Busy Day* (1800–1801) and *The Woman Hater* (1800–1801).

Although she is remembered as a novelist and diarist, Fanny Burney was also an extremely talented playwright. Her plays extend fully the natural genius for dramatisation which dominates her journals and contributed to the brilliance of *Evelina*. Her theatrical flair was immediately apparent to some of her most eminent admirers. 'I think, and say, she should write a comedy', was Sheridan's comment after the publication of *Evelina*, and 'She has certainly, something of a knack at character',[2] warmly agreed Sir Joshua Reynolds. But the thought of a theatre and the inevitable accompanying publicity terrified Burney. 'I actually shook from head to foot', she reported, on hearing their idea that she should write for the stage. 'I felt myself already in Drury Lane, amidst the hubbub of a first night'. Despite her trepidation, however, she yielded to their suggestions and began work almost at once on her first comedy, *The Witlings*.

Perhaps it was only in writing her plays that Fanny Burney found a public form in which she felt at home, for the technique of playwriting required no exposure of her personal voice. As she had done in *Evelina*, she was able to hide her own personality behind the comic utterances of others and could relax by letting her characters speak for themselves. *The Witlings* and the comedies which succeeded it owe a great deal to the conventions of eighteenth-century theatre. The plots are versions of those most popular at the time, of threatened disinheritance, mistaken identity and family estrangements and reconciliations. *The Witlings* has five acts, each containing one scene only, and its minimal plot – the heroine's sudden loss of fortune and consequent separation from and eventual reunion with the man she loves – is really just a gesture towards the formalities of structure. Burney's interest is in satire. The main focus of attack is on the parade of learning and her central characters are not romantic figures but buffoons who discredit themselves through their ignorance and pretentiousness. As their names suggest, Lady Smatter, Mrs Voluble, Mrs Sapient and the poet, Dabbler, are narrowly drawn but they are sharply executed. Burney had an acute ear for the subtleties of dialogue and she exploits skilfully the effects of comic juxtaposition of voices.

Significantly, her subject is women's learning. Lady Smatter has formed 'a kind of club at her house, professedly for the discussion of literary subjects, & the set who compose it are about as well qualified for the Purpose, as so many dirty Cabbin boys would be to find out the Longitude. To a very little reading, they join less understanding, & no judgement, yet they decide upon Books & Authors with the most confirmed confidence in their abilities for the Task.' The club, composed of 'authors & critics', bears an uncomfortable resemblance to the real-life Mrs Montagu's formidable society of *bas-bleus* and Burney is clearly suspicious of the motives behind such a project. 'I declare', announces Lady Smatter blithely, 'if my pursuits were not made public, I should not have any at all, for where can be the pleasure of reading Books, & studying Authors, if one is not to have the credit of talking of them.' Lady Smatter's speeches are peppered with misquotations and ostentatious references (wrongly attributed) to Shakespeare, Pope and Swift, the authors whom she most passionately loves to criticise because 'I have found more errors in those than in any other'. Lady Smatter is a savage portrait of intellectual affectation and it is hardly surprising that Dr Burney and Mr Crisp feared for Fanny's reputation if the play were to be performed. For *The Witlings* reveals Fanny Burney to be not the diffident, gentle creature her father and Crisp thought they had reared but an incisive satirist, relishing her own facility for viciousness. Her writing is direct and unafraid, basking in the force of the onslaught. 'Heavens', is one character's appalled comment on Lady Smatter, 'that a Woman whose utmost natural capacity will hardly enable her to understand the History of Tom Thumb, & whose comprehensive faculties would be absolutely baffled by the lives of the Champions of Christendom, should dare blaspheme the names of our Noblest Poets with words that convey no ideas, & sentences of which the sound listens in vain for the sense!'

Like Sheridan's Mrs Malaprop in *The Rivals*, Lady Smatter reflects the contemporary interest in language use and meaning and Burney's own feelings about the process and status of literary composition are given vent both in her lampoons of the superficially learned ladies and in her portrayal of the rhymster, Dabbler, remarkable only for his total lack of originality and his paucity of inventiveness. Called on to produce verse extempore, Dabbler reads out an obscure couplet of Pope's that he has prepared for just such an occasion, hoping to pass it off as his own, but he is floored by further requests to demonstrate his skill at poesy. In one scene he is shown in the mechanical act of poetic composition, desperately searching for rhymes, regardless of their sense. Throughout the play, Burney's concern with the activities of reading and writing is evident, as she asks how society can measure these in the scheme of both private and public lives. The play ends with a deftly ironic touch, when Lady Smatter, who holds the purse strings, is forced to give her blessing to the marriage of the parted lovers – she is threatened by public lampoons and scurrilous ballads on her name should she refuse and is bribed with promises of a panegyric and songs of triumph on her wisdom should she consent. The power of the printed word is nicely proved indomitable.

Although she was persuaded to withdraw the play from publication Fanny Burney remained fascinated by the subject of women's learning. She returned to it again and again in her novels and Lady Smatter herself reappears, in a somewhat toned-down version, in Burney's later play, *The Woman Hater*. This play exists only in manuscript form, probably still at revision stage, much of it written on the backs of address leaves from old letters and on spare canvassing sheets from *Camilla*. The woman hater of the title, the middle-aged Sir Roderick, has been turned against the sex after a painful experience in his youth with Lady Smatter, who jilted him in favour of a man who made his addresses to her in verse. The action of the play is more complex than *The Witlings* and a more subdued Lady Smatter takes only a minor role but her distorted emphasis on scholarship remains. It gives Burney a pretext for the venomous diatribes against women which issue from Sir Roderick at periodic intervals and the satire is directed as much at male prejudice as it is at female pedantry, as Sir Roderick recalls with bitterness his relationship with Lady Smatter.

> One day, when I wanted to see her, she sent me word she was finishing a new pamphlet! A woman reading a pamphlet! What could she understand of it? . . . Another time she sent me excuse she was writing a letter! Women writing letters! What can they have to say? . . . (on Pope and Shakespeare) – Women ought to be ashamed of talking such jargon. What can their little heads make out of such matters? What do they know? And what ought they to know? – except to sew a Gown, & make a pudding?

While Fanny Burney is clearly enjoying herself poking fun at such chauvinism, she is also enquiring more seriously into the place of education in women's lives, a topic that occupied her continually. Ignorance is openly condemned as the portrayal of the boisterous Miss Wilmot demonstrates. This gauche adolescent throws away her books and rejects study in favour of dancing, chattering and generally running wild. Suitably, she is paired at the end of the play with a man who is totally illiterate, the dunce, Bob Sapling, another survivor from *The Witlings*.

The Woman Hater is a composite of masculine prejudices about women. Carefully patterned, each element of the action has at its centre a woman who is misunderstood, whether it be the sad figure of the noble lady, Eleonora, deserted by her husband because of his unfounded suspicions about her fidelity, or the romantic innocent, Sophia, who is mistaken by an elderly rake for a prostitute, or the silly Miss Wilmot, whose true parentage has been kept a secret for the past seventeen years, or even the ridiculous Lady Smatter, who is erroneously taken by Sir Roderick as a deceptive paradigm for her sex. The themes of confused identities and disinheritance, which were fundamental to much eighteenth-century drama, are given a new twist by Burney when applied specifically to women, seen always struggling against the sexual stereotyping conferred on them by men.

Yet it is comedy which is Fanny Burney's forte and she does not allow herself to be tempted into romantic excess. On the contrary, she is exceptionally sensitive to the need to maintain consistency of tone. The final reconciliation scene of *The Woman Hater*, for example, becomes funny because of the fast-moving series of multiple revelations and recognitions. The serious business of restoring the long-separated husband with his forsaken wife and daughter is interspersed with the comic reunion between Sir Roderick and the now widowed Lady Smatter, who is proved still to have the power to rouse him to passion – although this veers erratically between love and fury. The element of pathos which threatens to intrude is deflated by the scenes with Sophia, the naive maiden, the epitome of feminine modesty. Timidly approaching a man she wrongly believes to be her uncle, she invites him to her cottage but her advances are grossly misinterpreted. In her plays, Burney does not hesitate to capitalise on the bawdy potential of situation. Men perceive women as occupying one extreme of a sexual role – Sophia is one minute spotless virgin and next scarlet temptress – but the suggestiveness is an occasion for humour and does not demolish the heroine's status. It is partly the economy of method that creates the effectiveness of such episodes but there is also a sense of licence here which is missing from Burney's novels, written to appeal to a largely female readership, growing increasingly prudish in its sensibilities.

The Woman Hater, *Love and Fashion* and *A Busy Day* were

all written in the years when Burney was freed from oppressive cares. Luxuriating in domestic felicity, at home in the comfortable and quiet Camilla Cottage, Fanny Burney was sufficiently relaxed to return to the mode she had been thwarted from exploring in her youth. She had a permanent interest in the theatre and recognised the special demands of performance. Her copy of *The Woman Hater* is notated at intervals with '6 minutes', '2 minutes', etc., indicating her alertness to the exigencies of staging and her memorandums and notebooks reveal a similar attentiveness to other technical constraints.

Many of her jottings contain scraps of dialogue that were never used, drafts for individual speeches, short synopses of plots or character descriptions. Her Mrs Megrim, for instance, is 'A Woman who sacrifices all forms, all appearances, all considerations to present sport, whim & fantastic humour: careless what is thought of her, & never so charmed as when the occasion of confusion & embarrassment'. Burney was absorbed by interaction and response between characters and in playwriting she found the perfect opportunity to turn this interest to account.

Love and Fashion and *A Busy Day* are comedies of manners that make full use of such theatrical effects and in particular the 'confusion & embarrassment' that Burney found so diverting. More conventional in the material they employ than *The Witlings* and *The Woman Hater*, they show Burney's unerring comic touch still as fresh and as hard hitting as it was in *Evelina* and her other early writings. Contrary to the evidence suggested by a reading of her novels, there is no sign of the slightest diminution of her literary gifts. *Love and Fashion* is a satire on the mercenary society and its unhealthy obsession with fashion, parade and vanity. The action follows the moral progress of the heroine, Hilaria, from her fascination with the delights of the town – jewellery, gaming, parties, the opera, gossip – to her acceptance of the pleasures of a country existence – peace, simplicity, pastoral beauty.

The writing is clearly influenced by Fanny Burney's own experience of rural bliss, when gardening was 'ecstasy' and she and D'Arblay could dine 'exquisitely' off boiled eggs, a new loaf and fresh water from their own well. Sentimentalism, however, is by no means allowed to dominate and the dialogue frequently has a Wildean brittleness and cynicism.

> *Miss Exbury*. But pray, now, do tell me – don't you think it amazingly odd that Sir Archy Fincer should come down to my Uncle Ardville's?
> *Hilaria*. Not at all. He's my cousin you know.
> *Miss Exbury*. How blind she is! as if people come to see their relations!

The dry realism which produces the play's main style is used to undercut any tendencies towards emotional exaggeration and the work forms in part a critique of Gothic extremism. When the impoverished Lord Exbury is forced to move from his stately dwelling, which he can no longer afford to keep, into a lonely cottage reputed to be haunted, fears of the supernatural become an occasion for farce not mystery. The only characters who believe in the ghosts are manifest fools and their terrors are never for a moment allowed to hold any credence with the audience.

A similar procedure is adopted in the more accomplished *A Busy Day* where the romantic interest provides the mechanism for the plot but where the gravity of the lovers is undercut when they become embroiled in the ludicrous confusions which surround them. It deals with the return from India of a genteel heiress, Eliza Watts, who has been brought up there by her adoptive father. On her arrival in London, she is immediately confounded by meeting her natural family, ill-bred, nouveau-riche 'Cits', whose plebeian behaviour is an embarrassing hindrance to her wish to marry into the aristocracy. The principal source of comedy lies in the collision between these vulgarians and the noble but snobbish family of Eliza's lover, Cleveland. The class levels and the language that belongs to each are sharply and subtly distinguished, so that it is the interplay of tones and manners which creates the dynamic of the text. Eliza's modesty and sentimental cast of mind, for instance, are gently mocked by being placed in a context where these qualities of refinement go for nothing. 'Well now, let's talk. Pray, how long have you had this lover?' familiarly enquires her new found sister. Eliza's reply is tastefully reserved, 'Pardon me, Sister, the narrative just now would extremely oppress me', but her dignified hauteur is wasted on Miss Watts whose response shatters all the rules of gentility.

> 'I want monstrously to see him. I intend, when you are married, you should *Shaproon* me everywhere, for I hate monstrously to go out with Ma! Don't you think Ma's monstrous mean? And Pa's so vulgar, you can't think how I'm ashamed of him. Do you know I was one day walking in the Park, with some young ladies I'd just made acquaintance with, quite the pelite sort, when all of a sudden I felt somebody twitch me by the elbow: so I screatched and called out, La, how impertinent! and when I turned round saying, do pray, Sir, be less free of your hands, who should I see but Pa.'

In the exposé of manners, Burney ridicules the foibles of both high-life and low-life characters with a range of superb cameos, from the uncouth Watts family (*Evelina*'s Branghtons resurrected) to the elegant flirt, Miss Percival, plus a redoubtable dowager, an antecedent of Wilde's Lady Bracknell, who scrutinises all newcomers as if they are candidates for admission into her family circle.

During the five long, miserable years that Burney spent at Court the spirit of gaiety that we find permeating these four comedies was dimmed and Burney turned instead to writing sombre verse tragedies, perhaps more in keeping with her state of mind. *Edwy and Elgiva*, *Hubert de Vere*, *The Siege of Pevensey* and the fragment, *Elberta*, were all begun in the lonely years 1788–91. Deprived of vivacity and stimulation in the life around her, Burney turned to historical sources for her inspiration and reworked extant material. Written at a time when Burney was dominated by her own sense of frustration and isolation, these dismal exercises in heroic drama deal yet again with female victimisation. Morbid women are unfairly treated, misjudged, confined, suffer and die in dreary circumstances. *Edwy and Elgiva* survived one disastrous performance only and we should perhaps be grateful for the natural demise of the rest. But the four comedies remain to testify to Burney's resilience and her enduring literary expertise. *A Busy Day*, in particular, is tightly constructed and easily sustains its glittering comic momentum throughout its five acts. In its adroit juxtaposition of personalities, styles and social mores it completely fulfils the promise of *Evelina*, albeit some twenty years late.

The journals and plays of Fanny Burney complement one another in showing us an alternative side to the increasingly restrained writer of the novels. They reveal a woman acutely observant and often outspoken in her opinions, candid and direct in her criticism of her contemporaries. They show too a woman obsessed with the process of literary composition, flexible and open to experiment, with a strong sense of artistic decorum, meticulous in her desire for perfection. 'What happened to a talent that augured so well?', a recent critic has asked, disappointed with the post-*Evelina* fiction. It is in Fanny Burney's journals and plays that we find the answer to that question.

8 Conclusion

In 1843, Macaulay wrote of Fanny Burney that when he heard the news of her death, 'all those whom we had been accustomed to revere as intellectual patriarchs seemed children when compared with her, for Burke had sate up all night to read her writings, and Johnson had pronounced her superior to Fielding when Rogers was still a schoolboy, and Southey still in petticoats'.[1] Ostensibly reviewing the initial publication of five volumes of her diaries and letters, Macaulay took the opportunity to review rather the nature of Burney's total achievement. His essay is still one of the most penetrating assessments we have. As befitted his time, his interest lay primarily in analysing the creative impulse but in his blending of biographical material with critical insights Macaulay pounced on the key to understanding the perplexing anomalies of Fanny Burney's writings.

For when we read the best of Burney's work – the satiric vignettes of *Evelina*, the vivid caricatures of *Cecilia*, the snappy comic scenes of *A Busy Day*, the emotional dramas of the letters – we can have no doubt that here was a woman of intelligence and discrimination, coupled with a natural gaiety and liveliness. Yet her complete oeuvre is inevitably a disappointment. Her novels, the work which made her famous, always promise more than they provide. The potential of her first book, *Evelina*, was never fully realised in her subsequent published work, although her literary career continued for fifty years afterwards. How can this be explained?

Perpetually readers have been intrigued by the idea of decline. 'The Retreat from Wonder' is how one recent critic has described Burney's 'literary falling-off'[2] in an essay addressed specifically to the phenomenon of her apparent regression. 'Fanny wrote better before she was married than since, however that came about',[3] observed Mrs Piozzi, perceptive as usual but not terribly helpful. As Macaulay commented, 'We have no reason to think that at a time when her faculties ought to have been in their maturity, they were smitten with any blight'. Macaulay was of course quite right. Burney's talents were not blighted at all but remained as glowing as ever throughout her life. Any reader of her journals can attest to that. Scrutiny should perhaps focus not so much on the idea of waning abilities but on the glaring and curious disparities between Burney's later published and unpublished writing.

The undeniable deterioration in quality of her novels when placed side by side with the sustained power of the journals and the zest of the plays, suggests in itself something about the problematic nature of Burney's relationship with her reading public, a relationship that is paradigmatic of the situation of women writers in the late eighteenth and early nineteenth centuries. Like most women of her time, brought up to respect irrevocable codes of behaviour, Fanny Burney had a deep and enduring need to win the approval of her family and her audience. Her life was formed on the principles of reaction and response rather than action and initiative. The act of publication per se was sufficiently daring for her to wish most fervently to remain within the bounds of modesty in other respects. Women were not yet so emancipated as to be able to risk alienating the sympathy of those on whom they depended for love and protection. As her novels show, Burney was fully aware of the difficulties attaching to the mirage of female independence. So her writing had its own inbuilt constraints. The psychological effects of the subsequent split between public persona and private self are forcefully dramatised in the dichotomy of Burney's literary output: the novels increasingly tense in style and secretive in method and the journals contrastingly open and immediate.

From the nineteenth century onwards, Burney's reputation has normally rested on the laurels brought her by the success of *Evelina*. *Cecilia* has come in for its faint share of praise but, in general, critics have dismissed the rest of Fanny Burney's work as unworthy of serious notice, subscribing resignedly to the notion of her diminishing powers. This theory has been widely accepted, even among her most committed fans. 'The disappearance of many of the qualities and felicities which had come to be expected from the author of *Evelina* . . . has never been wholly understood',[4] Joyce Hemlow remarked sadly. And this is perhaps why the major works devoted to Burney have so far been biographical and historical rather than critical.

Certainly no writer has offered richer material to would-be biographers than Fanny Burney, with her legacy of manuscripts, detailing so thoroughly her daily activities, thoughts and opinions; mingling shrewd comments on contemporary manners with bouts of self-analysis and moments of unguarded intimacy. As a chronicler of her age, she is incomparable and her authority as an informative source has been sought on topics ranging from musicology to procedure at the court of Queen Charlotte. To date, the standard biography is Joyce Hemlow's *The History of Fanny Burney* (1958), which sensitively interprets the mass of source material available – Burney's own journals and letters along with those of contemporaries, such as Mrs Thrale and Mrs Delaney – to provide a full and scholarly account of Burney's life and literary career. Hemlow isolates crucial periods in Burney's life to highlight distinct areas of her literary development. She devotes single chapters to each of the novels, to the plays and to the memoir of Dr Burney to place the literary productions in the context of information given by the journals. Her searching exegesis is augmented by two seminal articles, 'Fanny Burney, Playwright' (1948) and 'Fanny Burney and the Courtesy Books' (1950), which demonstrate convincingly Burney's debt to a variety of contemporary literary models.

The biography has been complemented recently by the exhaustive twelve volume collection of the *Journals and Letters of Fanny Burney*, also under the editorial supervision of Joyce Hemlow, in which the full scope and power of Burney's writing have become apparent to many readers for the first time. In making this journal material accessible, the editors have revealed a view of Fanny Burney that previously could only have been suspected by a particularly assiduous reader of her novels. Massively annotated and scrupulously organised, the edition of these diaries offers an insight into the latter years of Burney's life that has before been denied all but the most persevering scholars. In a review of Volumes XI and XII, Pat Rogers asked whether 'the letters will allow us to smuggle Fanny Burney into a more central place in literary history'.[5] Hopefully, they will do just that for they reveal an alternative side to the Burney coin that invites a revaluation of traditional critical estimates of her abilities.

Until recently, only minimal attention was paid by literary critics to the Burney canon. She was mentioned summarily in histories of the English novel as a lone figure of merit among many less skilful contemporaries, bridging the gap between Smollett and Jane Austen, with less verve than the one and less delicacy than the other. While most readers have been prepared to command Burney's gift for observation and her accuracy of delineation, these qualities have at the same time been brushed aside as a facile knack and critics have generally judged her on her limitations. David Cecil's view is all too typical of opinion up to the middle of the twentieth century that 'the novel to her was not the expression of an imaginative conception, but merely a means of recording her observations of the world, which she organised into an artificial unity by using any convention of story-writing she found to her hand'.[6] 'Her range was limited . . . conventional and unimaginative',[7] agreed traditionalists disparagingly. Yet J. M. S. Tompkins, in her wide ranging account of the character and fortunes of the popular novel in England in the last years of the eighteenth century, recognised that Fanny Burney was far more than a clever concocter drawing on prevailing trends. For Burney, although not wholly escaping the formality and artifice of her time amidst a current vogue for sensationalism, remained cool and focused on characters and actions that were essentially familiar. Her plots and situations were not outrageous but reasonable and, as Tompkins commented, 'the future lay with them'.[8]

Mostly, Fanny Burney has gained credit in the shadow of her more famous successor, Jane Austen, whose novels came swiftly on the heels of *Evelina* and *Cecilia*. Frank Bradbrook in *Jane Austen and her Predecessors* cites Burney's writing as the principal model for Austen's fiction, for while Austen's style has 'greater range, flexibility and complexity', the influence of Burney is unmistakable, even when it is only used to provide material for burlesque. Bradbrook tends to concentrate on the more mechanical aspects of the relationship between the two writers, their stylistic similarities, their common source in Johnson and Fielding, the parallelism of certain scenes, such as the proposal scenes in *Cecilia* and *Pride and Prejudice*, echoes in subjects of conversation – dancing is his prime example – and character borrowings – the silent Miss Leeson and the voluble Miss Larolles from *Cecilia* are neatly compared with *Emma*'s Jane Fairfax and Miss Bates.[9] Working along similar lines, Kenneth Moler has pointed out interesting affinities between *Evelina* and *Pride and Prejudice*.[10] His emphasis is on the conception of the patrician hero, a dominant figure in the fiction of both writers, and a creation which, as Tompkins has remarked, suggests the deep need of women of that time to escape from the world of male crudity to a world of refinement and gentility. When David Cecil observed succinctly that Fanny Burney's novels marked the entry of the lady into English fiction, he too was acknowledging the move from action to introspection that became such a salient feature of women's writing at this period.

For whatever their estimation of her achievement, critics have concertedly recognised that Burney's gender has been a controlling and distinctive factor in her approach. 'Her appearance is an important epoch in our literary history', Macaulay declared unhesitatingly, because 'Evelina was the first tale written by a woman, and purporting to be a picture of life and manners, that lived or deserved to live'. In showing life 'though a woman's eyes' Fanny Burney paved the way for the women writers that were to follow her, and with the growth of feminist criticism in the second half of the twentieth century new interest has been generated in her work as readers have been alerted to the significance of her alternative view of experience.

In this light it can be seen that Fanny Burney was not just amalgamating the devices and conventions she found in the literature around her. Both in content and in form her novels differ from those of her male predecessors. Her subjects are women's lives and the special problems they embrace. She presents the apparent trivia with which women are surrounded and their attempt to construct meaning from impedimenta. With increasing vehemence she shows their enforced observance to a code of behaviour which is frequently at odds with the urge for individual expression. These issues are crucial in Burney's novels and as she became more self-conscious about her art she sought ways of formulating her misgivings, unable to dismiss sympathies which were often in conflict with the principles of order to which she was committed. The use of comedy as a protective mechanism served Burney well for the portrayal of potentially subversive characters, such as Mrs Selwyn, or for apparently meliorating her deprecating opinion of the male hierarchy.

Several critics have noted the elements of discordance in

Burney's work and the lesser known novels have proved
fruitful territory for discerning readers. A number of articles
have appeared in scholarly journals, dealing with individual
texts, which throw valuable light on Burney's concern with
incipient feminist issues; the education of girls in *Camilla*,
doctrines of female emancipation in *The Wanderer*, the crisis
of identity in *Evelina*.[11] The growing credibility of women's
studies has facilitated new readings of Burney's work,
especially with reference to the construction of a female
literary tradition. Eva Figes, for instance, in a stimulating
discussion, has shown the importance of Burney's
contribution to the reshaping of the English novel with the
advent of women writers.[12] And Katharine Rogers, in her
study of feminism in eighteenth-century England, places
Burney's dramatisation of women's helplessness in a wider
context of female fear of reprisal and struggle for articulacy.[13]

The ambivalence which is at the heart of Burney's writing
has been most probingly considered by Patricia Meyer
Spacks. Examining the struggles around which Burney's
novels pivot and the overriding concern with the heroine's
anxieties, she concludes that 'The feeling heart guarantees
misery; only by emotional repression can a woman survive
successfully in a world which penalizes female
expressiveness'.[14] Fanny Burney's novels are about women's
suffering, and their own ability to shield their precarious
sense of identity. This is the idea which has given shape to
Spacks's Imagining A Self (1976), the only work to appear so
far which seriously investigates the implications of women's
private and confessional writings. In a chapter entitled 'The
Dynamics of Fear' Spacks analyses the diaries' reliance on
techniques of concealment and suggests the close
correspondence between Burney's journals and her fiction.[15]
In her insistence on virtuous conduct, she argues, Burney is
establishing a defensive position which holds good for all
women. Her impeccable morality is a front, behind which
she is able to protect her inner life. It is in Burney's novels

that the guide lines for female survival are laid down for future writers to follow.

In their dynamic study of the nineteenth century, *The Madwoman in the Attic* (1979), Sandra Gilbert and Susan Gubar argue that women writers were dogged by myths of female licence as female evil and consequently developed sophisticated techniques of subterfuge in order to contain their impulses to rebellion.[16] For us to understand the ways in which women artists of the nineteenth century dealt with the subjects of female power, female silence, duty and self-realisation, we must look to their eighteenth-century progenitor. Fanny Burney was a quiet and original pioneer of the strategies of dissension which found their most penetrating exponents in the great women novelists of the next generation, Jane Austen, Charlotte Brontë, Elizabeth Gaskell and George Eliot. She did not rampantly challenge the conventions which bound her but found instead secretive ways to work within them and turn them to advantage. The inconsistency in style between the journals and the fiction testifies compellingly to what Spacks has called the 'characteristic psychic conflict' that besets women writers.

'It was delightful to read a man's writing again', wrote Virginia Woolf about the mysterious Mr A. in *A Room of One's Own*. 'It was so direct, so straightforward after the writing of women. It indicated such freedom of mind, such liberty of person, such confidence in himself . . . this well-nourished, well-educated, free mind, which had never been thwarted or opposed, but had had full liberty from birth to stretch itself in whatever way it liked.'[17] How different from Fanny Burney! Unlike Woolf's Mr A. she wrote in an atmosphere of restriction and denial where free expression for women was suspicious and dangerous. The established tradition was of little real help to her in conveying her experience of the world and she had to discover her own methods of presenting her unique perceptions. In making women's lives a respectable subject for literature, Fanny

Burney also hit upon a way of writing that incorporated both endorsement and criticism of the confines within which she operated. In a consideration of the complete oeuvre, we see the growth of a double-edged vision of things, an indicator of the inhibited pen, which must seek underhand techniques of expression. Struggling to express herself, Fanny Burney initiated a whole tradition of women's writing.

Notes

Extracts from Burney's diaries and letters are taken from the following editions:

The Early Diary of Frances Burney 1768–1778 (2 vols), ed. Annie Raine Ellis (London, 1889)
The Diary of Fanny Burney, ed. Lewis Gibbs (Dent, 1971)
The Journals and Letters of Fanny Burney 1791–1840 (12 vols), eds Joyce Hemlow, Althea Douglas, Warren Derry et al. (Clarendon Press, 1972–1984)

Extracts from Fanny Burney's works are taken from the following editions:

Evelina (Dent, 1909)
Cecilia (Payne and Cadell, 1782)
Camilla (Oxford University Press, 1983)
The Wanderer (Longmans, 1814)
A Busy Day (Rutgers University Press, 1984)

Notes to Chapter 1

1. Quoted by R. B. Utter and G. B. Needham in *Pamela's Daughters* (Dixon, 1937), pp. 29–30.

2. Dr John Gregory, *A Father's Legacy to His Daughters* (Cadell, 1814), pp. 37–38.

3. Quoted by R. B. Utter and G. B. Needham in *Pamela's Daughters* (Dixon, 1937), p. 30.

4. *The Correspondents, An Original Novel*, 1775, quoted by J. M. S. Tompkins in *The Popular Novel in England 1770–1800* (Constable & Co., 1932) p. 127.

5. Charlotte Palmer, *Letters Upon Several Subjects from a Preceptress to her Pupils who have Left School* (1797), quoted by J. M. S. Tompkins in *The Popular Novel in England 1710–1800* (Constable & Co., 1932), p. 147.

6. Burney, *Diary* and Boswell, *Life of Johnson*, quoted by Katharine M. Rogers in *Feminism in Eighteenth-Century England* (University of Illinois Press, 1982), p. 27.

7. *Memoirs of Doctor Burney*, quoted by Joyce Hemlow in *The History of Fanny Burney* (Oxford University Press, 1958), p. 9.

8. Tobias Smollett, *The Expedition of Humphry Clinker* (The Modern Library, 1929), p. 69.

9. Burney, *The Wanderer* (Longmans, 1814), Introduction.

10. *Thraliana: the Diary of Mrs. Hester Lynch Thrale 1776–1809*, ed. Katharine C. Balderston (Clarendon Press, 1942), p. 916.

11. Jane Austen, *Persuasion* (Dent, 1962), p. 201.

12. *Critical* May 1793, p. 44, quoted by J. M. S. Tompkins in *The Popular Novel in England 1770–1800* (Constable & Co., 1932). Note to p. 71.

13. Sarah Fielding, *The Governess* (Oxford University Press, 1968), p. 87.

14. *The Example; or the History of Lucy Cleveland*, 1778, quoted by J. M. S. Tompkins in *The Popular Novel in England 1770–1800* (Constable & Co., 1932), p. 117.

15. Charlotte Smith, *Emmeline or the Orphan of the Castle* (Oxford University Press, 1971), p. 236.

16. Mary Wollstonecraft, *A Vindication of the Rights of Women* (Dent, 1975), Ch. IV.

17. Letter to Horace Walpole, quoted by K. Rogers in *Feminism in Eighteenth-Century England* (University of Illinois Press, 1982), p. 209.

Notes to Chapter 2

1. Quoted by R. B. Utter and G. B. Needham in *Pamela's Daughters* (Dixon, 1937) p. 34.

2. Hester Chapone, *Letters on the Improvement of the Mind* (1773) quoted by K. Rogers in *Feminism in Eighteenth-Century England* (University of Illinois Press, 1982), p. 214.

3. Mary Wollstonecraft, *Mary, A Fiction* (Clarendon Press, 1976) Ch. 24, p. 53.

4. William Hazlitt, *Lectures on the English Comic Writers*, 'Mme. D'Arblay' in *The Complete Works of William Hazlitt*, ed. Howe, (Dent, 1931), p. 123.

5. Patricia Meyer Spacks, *Imagining a Self* (Harvard University Press, 1976), pp. 158–92.

Notes to Chapter 3

1. This and the following opinions on *Evelina* are quoted in Burney's *Early Diary*, ed. Annie Raine Ellis (Bell, 1907), pp. 220–49, Vol. II.

2. Virginia Woolf, 'Modern Fiction', *The Common Reader I* (Hogarth Press, 1925).

3. Sandra Gilbert and Susan Gubar, *The Madwoman in the Attic: The Woman Writer and the Nineteenth-Century Imagination* (Yale University Press, 1979).

Notes to Chapter 4

1. Quoted by Constance Hill in *Juniper Hall* (John Lane, 1904) and Joyce Hemlow, *The History of Fanny Burney* (Oxford University Press, 1959), p. 157.

2. Letter from Edmund Burke to Miss F. Burney 29 July 1782, quoted in *The Diary of Fanny Burney*, ed. L. Gibbs, pp. 78–79.

3. Roy Porter, *English Society in the Eighteenth-Century* (Penguin, 1982), p. 40.

4. Eliza Haywood, *The Female Spectator* (1774), quoted by Mary R. Mahl and Helene Koon in *The Female Spectator* (Indiana University Press, 1977), p. 234.

5. Frances Brooke, *Lady Julia Mandeville* (Dodsley, 1763), p. 42.

6. Charlotte Smith, *Emmeline* (Oxford University Press, 1971), pp. 122–23.

7. Anna Laetitia Barbauld, Letter to Mrs Montagu (c. 1774) and Letter 'On Female Studies', quoted by M. R. Mahl and H. Koon in *The Female Spectator* (Indiana University Press, 1977), pp. 262 and 271.

8. Frances Brooke, *Lady Emily Montague* (Dodsley, 1769).

Notes to Chapter 5

1. 'Camilla, by Mrs. D'Arblay', The *British Critic* 1796, p. 536.

2. Elizabeth Inchbald, *A Simple Story* (Oxford University Press, 1967), p. 338.

3. Lady Sarah Pennington, *An Unfortunate Mother's Advice to her Absent Daughters* (1761), quoted by Frank Bradbrook in *Jane Austen and her Predecessors* (Cambridge University Press, 1967), Appendix II, pp. 143–54.

4. 'Mrs. D'Arblay's Camilla', The *Monthly Review* 1796, Vol. XXI, p. 163.

5. Mary Wollstonecraft, *A Vindication* (Penguin, 1978), p. 103.

6. Hannah More, *Strictures on the Modern System of Female Education* (Garland, 1974).

Notes to Chapter 6

1. Croker, 'D'Arblay's Wanderer', The *Quarterly Review* xi April 1814, pp. 123–30.

2. *Ibid.*

3. H. *Theatrical Inquisitor and Monthly Mirror*, April 1814, pp. 234–37.

4. Mary Wollstonecraft, *A Vindication* (Dent, 1975), Ch. IV.

5. Quoted by Claire Tomalin in *The Life and Death of Mary Wollstonecraft* (Penguin, 1974), p. 52.

Notes to Chapter 7

1. Jane Austen, *Northanger Abbey*, (Dent, 1962), Ch. III, pp. 12–13.

2. Quoted in Fanny Burney, *Early Diary*.

Notes to Chapter 8

1. Macaulay, *The Edinburgh Review*, Jan. 1843, Vol. LXXVI.

2. Lillian D. and Edward A. Bloom, 'Fanny Burney's Novels: The Retreat from Wonder', *Novel* (Spring, 1979).

3. *Autobiography, Letters and Literary Remains of Mrs. Piozzi*, ed. A. Hayward (Longmans, 1861).

4. Joyce Hemlow, 'Fanny Burney and the Courtesy Books', *PMLA* 65 (1950), pp. 732–61.

5. *The Times Literary Supplement*, 4 Jan. 1985, p. 8.

6. Lord David Cecil, 'Fanny Burney's Novels', *Poets and Storytellers* (Constable & Co., 1949).

7. Walter Allen, *The English Novel* (Penguin, 1954), p. 95; Harrison R. Steeves, *Before Jane Austen* (Allen & Unwin, 1966), p. 218.

8. J. M. S. Tompkins, *The Popular Novel in England 1770–1800* (Constable & Co., 1932) p. 60.

9. Frank Bradbrook, *Jane Austen and her Predecessors* (Cambridge University Press, 1966), pp. 94–102.

10. Kenneth Moler, *Jane Austen's Art of Allusion* (University of Nebraska Press, 1977). Also, 'Fanny Burney's Cecilia and Jane Austen's Jack and Alice', *English Language Notes* 3, 1965, pp. 40–42.

11. Coral Ann Howells, 'The Proper Education of a Female . . . Is Still to Seek', *British Journal for Eighteenth-Century Studies*, Vol. 7, No. 2, Autumn 1984, pp. 191–98; Rose Marie Cutting, 'A Wreath for Fanny Burney's Last Novel', *Illinois Quarterly*, 1975, pp. 45–64; Jill Rubenstein, 'The Crisis of Identity in Fanny Burney's Evelina', *New Rambler* 1972, pp. 45–50.

12. Eva Figes, *Sex and Subterfuge. Women Writers to 1850* (Macmillan, 1982).

13. Katharine Rogers, *Feminism in Eighteenth-Century England* (University of Illinois Press, 1982).

14. Patricia Meyer Spacks, 'Ev'ry Woman is at Heart a Rake', *Eighteenth-Century Studies* Fall 1974, pp. 27–46.

15. Patricia Meyer Spacks, *Imagining A Self. Autobiography and the Novel in Eighteenth-Century England* (Harvard University Press, 1976).

16. Sandra Gilbert and Susan Gubar, *The Madwoman in the Attic: The Woman Writer and the Nineteenth-Century Imagination* (Yale University Press, 1979).

17. Virginia Woolf, *A Room of One's Own* (Hogarth Press, 1928), p. 98.

Bibliography

Published Works by Fanny Burney (D'Arblay)

Evelina (Oxford University Press, 1970).
Cecilia (Virago, 1986).
Camilla (Oxford University Press, 1972).
The Wanderer (Longmans, 1814).
A Busy Day (Rutgers University Press, 1984).
Memoirs of Doctor Burney (Moxon, 1832).
The Early Diary of Frances Burney 1768–1778, edited by Annie Raine Ellis (Bell, 1907).
The Diary of Fanny Burney, edited by Lewis Gibbs (Everyman, Dent, 1971).
The Diary and Letters of Madame D'Arblay, edited by Austin Dobson (Macmillan, 1904).
The Journals and Letters of Fanny Burney (Madame D'Arblay) 1791–1840: Vols I–VI, edited by Joyce Hemlow with Patricia Boutilier and Althea Douglas; Vol. VII, edited by Edward A. and Lillian D. Bloom; Vol. VIII, edited by Peter Hughes; Vols IX and X, edited by Warren Derry; Vols XI and XII, edited by Joyce Hemlow with Althea Douglas and Patricia Hawkins (Oxford University Press, 1972–1984).

Selected Biographical and Critical Studies of Fanny Burney

Adelstein, Michael, *Fanny Burney* (Shoestring Press, 1968).
Bloom, Lillian D. and Edward A., 'Fanny Burney's Novels: The Retreat from Wonder', *Novel: A Forum on Fiction* 12 (1979), pp. 215–35.
Cecil, David, Lord, 'Fanny Burney's Novels', *Poets and Storytellers* (Constable & Co., 1949).

Cutting, Rose Marie, 'A Wreath for Fanny Burney's Last Novel', *Illinois Quarterly* (1975), pp. 45–64; 'Defiant Women: The Growth of Feminism in Fanny Burney's Novels', *Studies in English Literature* 17 (1977), pp. 519–30.

Gerin, Winifred, *The Young Fanny Burney* (Thomas Nelson, 1961).

Gran, Joseph A., *Fanny Burney: An Annotated Bibliography* (Garland, 1981).

Hahn, Emily, *A Degree of Prudery* (Barker, 1950).

Hemlow, Joyce, *The History of Fanny Burney* (Oxford University Press, 1958). 'Fanny Burney and the Courtesy Books', *PMLA* 65 (1950), pp. 732–61: 'Fanny Burney, Playwright', *University of Toronto Quarterly* xix (1950), pp. 70–89.

Howells, Coral Ann, 'The Proper Education of a Female . . . Is Still to Seek', *British Journal for Eighteenth-Century Studies* 17 (1984), pp. 191–98.

Kilpatrick, Sarah, *Fanny Burney* (David and Charles, 1980).

Rubenstein, Jill, 'The Crisis of Identity in Fanny Burney's Evelina', *New Rambler* 12 (1972), pp. 45–50.

Spacks, Patricia Meyer, 'The Dynamics of Fear', *Imagining A Self* (Harvard University Press, 1976); 'Ev'ry Woman is at Heart a Rake', *Eighteenth-Century Studies* (Fall 1974), pp. 27–46.

White, Eugene, *Fanny Burney, Novelist: A Study in Technique* (Shoestring, 1960).

Works on the Social, Historical and Cultural Background of Women of the Period

Backsheider, Paula R., 'Woman's Influence', *Studies in the Novel* xi (Spring 1979), pp. 3–19.

Bradbrook, Frank, *Jane Austen and her Predecessors* (Cambridge University Press, 1966).

Doody, Margaret Anne, 'Deserts, Ruins and Troubled Waters: Female Dreams in Fiction and the Development of the Gothic Novel', *Genre* 10 (Winter 1977), pp. 529–72.

Figes, Eva, *Sex and Subterfuge. Women Writers to 1850* (Macmillan, 1982).

Fritz, Paul, and Morton, Richard (eds), *Women in the 18th Century and Other Essays* (Garland, 1976).

Kirkham, Margaret, *Jane Austen, Feminism and Fiction* (Harvester, 1982).

MacCarthy, B. G., *Later Women Novelists 1744–1818* (Cork University Press, 1947).

Mahl, Mary R., and Koon, Helene (eds), *The Female Spectator* (Indiana University Press, 1977).

Mews, Hazel, *Frail Vessels* (Athlone Press, 1969).

Moers, Ellen, *Literary Women* (The Womens Press, 1977).

Rogers, Katharine, *Feminism in Eighteenth-Century England* (University of Illinois Press, 1982).

Steeves, Edna L., 'Pre-Feminism in Some Eighteenth-Century Novels', *Texas Quarterly* 16 (Autumn 1973), pp. 48–57.

Steeves, Harrison R., *Before Jane Austen* (Allen and Unwin, 1966).

Thraliana: The Diary of Mrs. Hester Lynch Thrale 1776–1809, ed. Katharine C. Balderston (Clarendon Press, 1942).

Todd, Janet (ed.), *A Dictionary of British and American Women Writers 1660–1800* (Methuen & Co, 1984).

Tompkins, J. M. S., *The Popular Novel in England 1770–1800* (Constable & Co, 1932).

Utter, R. B., and Needham, G. B., *Pamela's Daughters* (Dixon, 1937).

Wollstonecraft, Mary, *A Vindication of the Rights of Women* (Dent, 1975).

Index

150